PRIME MINISTER
MODI's
GOVERNMENT OF BHARAT 2024

CHANGE → DEVELOPMENT → FUTURE

Karthik Thirunarayanan

INDIA · SINGAPORE · MALAYSIA

ISBN 979-8-89277-614-1

Contents

Foreword

I have shared a strong bond with the author for many years through his Commitment, selfless service, patriotism & contribution to the Nation. He is a person with great knowledge of good governance & I could see very few people who can passionately talk, discuss & share factual information about various initiatives & schemes of our Hon'ble Prime Minister Shri. Narendra Modi. Being an admirer of PM Modi & his excellent delivery of "Good Governance & Development", I get enlightened whenever the author shares key aspects of PM Modi's Good Governance Model during our conversations.

I always make sure to gain some knowledge from him so that I can share with my circle of people about Hon'ble PM Modi's good Governance & Government.

The author's commitment to writing this book is laudable. Despite his professional work, social services & other engagements, he could write this book only because of his passion for PM Modi's model of Good Governance. This book covers the election manifesto promises made & delivered by PM Modi government in the past successful ten years. The precise details mentioned in this book are eye-opening for me to understand the commitment of the Modi government to deliver the promises.

This book covers Term 1 (2014-2019) & term 2 (2019-2024) delivery of good governance & need for Modi Governance in 2024 for a better future. The book covers in detail how this Government is under the leadership of Hon'ble Prime Minister Shri. Narendra Modi delivered every promise he made in the manifesto. I was surprised to see the 360-degree analysis of PM Modi, who envisioned how the Nation could be empowered way back in 2014.

It is our duty & responsibility to read this book of at least two pages daily to understand how our great Nation has transformed in 10 years under the leadership of Hon'ble Prime Minister Shri. Narendra Modi. Exceptional services were delivered, empowering common people, including the poor, farmers, women, youth & children across all communities.

World leaders should read this book to understand the various development initiatives & schemes that can even be adopted by their respective Govt for delivering such good governance.

As a responsible citizen, I will ensure all my group organisations & friends read this book to gain awareness & knowledge about these various initiatives taken by PM Modi for our better future.

Dr. Ishari K. Ganesh
Founder & Chancellor – Vels University (VISTAS)

Let us remember and pay tribute to the
three stalwarts who served as pillars of strength & support for PM Modi.

Late Smt. Sushma Swaraji Ji,
Shri. Arun Jaitley Ji &
Shri. Manohar Parrikar Ji.

The level of commitment, courage & contribution from them cannot be measured, as patriotism is non-measurable. Nation first attitude with people welfare-focused services was only their daily agenda. When the nation was looking with hope & expectation in 2014 under the leadership of Hon'ble Prime Minister Shri. Narendra Modi, they ensured every step, initiative, and mission is delivered to protect & empower the common people of our great Nation – Bharat.

Smt. Sushma Swaraj Ji

Mother for all Bhartiya's living abroad said, *"I do not sleep, and I do not let Indian envoys sleep.* "She is the first External affairs minister who used social media & responded promptly 24/7 to overseas people of Bharat for any support. The respect & value of our nation & people changed across the globe due to her "My Nation, My People" attitude.

Shri. Arun Jaitley Ji

A person with perfection, strong & experienced legal acumen, intellect & legendary in the field of economy. His immense contribution to building our nation's economic foundation deserves a salute. Many fundamental economic & tax reforms (GST, IBC, Banks, Demonetisation) have helped give a strong foundation for our nation to progress towards the path of development.

Shri. Manohar Parrikar Ji

The first IIT-ian to become a Chief Minister and the country's Defence Minister. His simplicity and common man lifestyle made him the most admired Chief Minister of Goa. His contribution to our proud nation's defence forces is remarkable, with a dedication to empowering our armed forces with strength & strong muscle power. Implementation of OROP, the surgical strike and the modernisation of the armed forces were delivered during his tenure.

Acknowledgment

The details listed in this book were referred to from various publicly available websites of central government ministries and online media. The intention is to ensure every citizen in our proud nation - Bharat, has awareness, & gains knowledge about such wonderful people welfare-focused initiatives delivered by our people welfare-focused Prime Minister Shri. Narendra Modi.

I wish to sincerely thank all Hon'ble central government ministers, Bureaucrats, Hon'ble Chief Ministers of all States, Hon'ble state Ministers, officers & staff of both central and state governments' public sector units for their dedicated efforts and contributions to empowering every citizen under the leadership of Hon'ble Prime Minister Shri. Narendra Modi in the last 10 years.

Author's Note

BHARAT is a proud nation that served as the birthplace of culture, tradition, respect, human values, science, healthcare, technology, trade, economics, and education. There are many countries with old civilizations, but Bharat has always been the source of inspiration for humanity. Our ancient ancestors created Bharat as the planet's largest, oldest & wealthiest civilization; the entire world followed & learned from our principles. If there's one place where all of humanity's dreams have found a home from the earliest days of existence, it's Bharat.

"India is the cradle of the human race, the birthplace of human speech, the mother of history, the grandmother of legend, and the great grand mother of tradition. Our most valuable and most constructive materials in the history of man are treasured up in India only."

– *Mark Twain (American Writer)*

In Ramayana, Bhagavan Ram said to Lakshman, "Mother & Motherland is better than heaven."

Devotion can only be cultivated if one knows the glory & contribution of the motherland.

I am an ordinary citizen like you all. Born in a humble family. My father was a truck driver & who always believed only an ordinary person could understand the pain of the poor. During my school vacation days, my father used to take me along with him in the truck. I used to see the challenges he used to face & asked him, "When will this Change?".

My father said, "At least in your lifetime, I hope an ordinary person from a humble background will lift our nation toward development."

I feel honored to say today I could see the reality after 10 years of dedicated leadership under Hon'ble People's Prime Minister Shri. Narendra Modi.

My first book was authored in November 2018, "Architect of New India". I wish to share what made me write that book. In mid-2018, we were traveling from Bareilly (Uttar Pradesh) to Kanpur by road & and stopped our car to have a tea break. My friends chose to have tea & since I do not drink tea/coffee, I spotted a small fruit shop in that small location. The fruit shop was managed by a woman (in her 40s) who looked elated to see a customer coming to buy fruits. The fruit shop was a tiny, small location with lots of bananas & few other fruits. My eyes became curious when I saw a photo of Hon'ble Prime Minister Shri. Narendra Modi is next to God Shiva. I asked that woman if she was a BJP party worker; She replied, "No." again, I asked her whether someone from her family was in the BJP party post, and she replied, "No." Again, I asked, "are you a fan of Modi Ji," she replied "No." Then I asked her the reason behind keeping PM Modi's photo. The woman replied," I have 2 daughters (one in 11th standard & one in 9th Std). There was no toilet in our home & also school. Girl children needed to go out in the fields, which was a big challenge & insecure in many ways, especially in villages. Also, my kids could not go to school regularly because of these challenges.

Now I can proudly say my kids are studying well & I am feeling secure because there is a toilet in my home as well as at school. This could happen because we have PM Modi, who understands our women's problem. When we request God, a person blessed by God comes to support & resolve our problems. I see PM Modi as a God-blessed person. So PM Modi is a person whom I value next to God."

Her response made me feel more responsible as a citizen to take this "Change" across people. For many of us living in cities, this may be nothing, but when a PM could understand the pain & deliver change, we all should feel proud of this good governance under PM Modi's government.

The difference between an ordinary person and an extraordinary person is his thinking ability, passion for delivering & commitment to achieving. The goal of – Hon'ble Prime Minister Shri. Narendra Modi is **DEVELOPMENT & NATION FIRST** Policy.

We have a patriotic Prime Minister who treats 140 Cr people of our proud nation as his family.

A Prime Minister of a proud nation like ours should be a patriotic, passionate, committed, dedicated, brave, bold, visionary & people welfare-focused person who can deliver & share with pride about our nation's potential. After Atal Bihari Vajpayee Ji, I am honored to see all these qualities in our Hon'ble Prime Minister Modi.

In his 23 years of public service (13 years as Chief Minister & 10 years as Prime Minister), Shri. Narendra Modi is the first person to continuously serve & contribute maximum welfare initiatives in public services for the Development & Progress of our proud nation.

Before becoming Prime Minister of Bharat, Shri Narendra Modi was the Chief Minister of Gujarat for 13 years. He donated his entire 13 years of CM salary & auctioned all the gifts he received and contributed the entire money for girl child education & welfare.

In our daily lives, we, the common people, expect quality, eligibility & honesty in every aspect of our needs.

We expect **quality** even in a glass of water.

We expect **eligibility** in every public service.

We expect **honesty** from everyone.

But how many of us really think that a quality, eligible & honest, values-based government should only empower our nation?

Yes. Common people felt the same in 2014 and 2019 & elected the Modi government. We need to do the same for 3rd term to have a strong Modi government in 2024.

Let us see how this government, in their 2 consecutive terms, delivered Change & Development as promised in their Election Manifesto of 2014 & 2019.

I tried to capture the poll promises & the on-ground works delivered in almost the last 10 years of their dedicated services to the people of Bharat.

– Karthik Thirunarayanan

Modi Government – Term 1 (2014 – 2019) – Delivered Change

Bharat's Challenges Before 2014

Bharat Mata – A proud Nation with one of the oldest civilizations, which gave birth to many great religions, faiths, rich cultures & patriotic leaders. Before May 2014, Bharat's image on the world stage was stained with the color of corruption, lack of leadership, poor investment, slow development, lack of vision for the nation, missing concrete strategy for Domestic growth, and fragile relations with countries & developed Nations.

Bharat, to become a developed nation like the USA, China, Japan, Germany, and Australia & to become a powerful nation, needs to create a vibrant economic scenario, investment-friendly environment, strong bonding, gain trust, and improve relationships across major developed and countries - this was urgently needed to be addressed on TOP PRIORITY.

Poor People

After independence, our nation had great expectations for transformation, especially for poor people. The empowerment of poor people was just a dream kept alive by politicians who ensured their families and relatives alone were empowered. Poor people's ambition remained only on paper - every hard work of the poor, their earnings, and their future.

The poor remained poor because their benefits were looted, development was destroyed, and support was stopped. This continued for many decades. Their expectation faded & and they were in the ICU. More than 40% of our country's poor could not even have a bank account.

Farmers are the lifeline of our country. Agriculture is the primary source of livelihood for 58% of Bharat's population. As per the agriculture census, small and marginal holdings of less than 2 hectares account for 85% of total operational holdings of farming land. Poor farmers faced many challenges & hardships, which hampered their daily lives. Intermediaries looted poor farmers' hard work.

Rural Development never had a priority focus for a decade & villages could not transform.

One of the most critical requirements for poor people is affordable healthcare. The majority of the population lacked access to primary health care systems, mainly in rural areas. Many people, especially the poor & women, die due to the absence of "affordable health care." The healthcare system of Bharat lacked good governance for the delivery of health care for the poor.

Many low-income families could not access critical healthcare facilities, and substantial medical expenses further pushed their poverty down.

Children & Women

Children are the future of our Bharat. There were many challenges like child protection, elimination of child marriage and child labor, child survival, preventing neonatal death and stunting, eliminating open defecation, and providing quality education. For many decades, such focus areas were not taken on priority.

Children's' views, especially those of girls, children from disadvantaged groups, and marginalized communities, were affected due to a lack of judicial and administrative focus. Child sexual abuse needs a strict law to counter and punish such culprits severely.

Women are the backbone of the nation & pillars of Development Bharat. But their empowerment always moved at the slowest pace with the least importance. In Bharat, many poor women & children suffer due to a lack of adequate toilets. In fact, many girls drop out of school due to a lack of toilets, especially in rural areas. A report by the international charity said more than 56% of Bharat citizens lacked access to basic sanitation.

Bharat is home to more than 24 Crore households, out of which about 10 Crore households are still deprived of LPG as cooking fuel and must rely on firewood, coal, dung–cakes, etc. as the primary source of cooking. Smoke inhaled by women from unclean fuel is equivalent to burning 400 cigarettes in an hour.

Youth

Many centuries ago, our great nation served as a center for "youth empowerment" for the entire world. Bharat's great ancient universities like Takshashila, Nalanda, Mithila, Telhara, Sharada,

Vikramashila, Valabhi, and Somapura acted as "Youth Empowerment Hubs" across the world.

Youths are the roots of our great nation & their dedication and commitment contributed in a big way to build our nation. Youth icons like great warriors Chhatrapati Shivaji Maharaj, Swami Vivekananda, Veer Savarkar, Keshav Baliram Hedgewar, Subhash Chandra Bose, Mahakavi Bharathiyar, and Tiruppur Kumaran sacrificed their youth lives to build our nation through their selfless services.

Youths in Bharat represent the most dynamic & vibrant segment of our population. While most developed countries face the risk of an aging workforce, our nation has the world's largest youth population.

But Bharat's youth talent pool did not have opportunities for growth, lacked self-employment opportunities, no skill development, no startup platforms for talented youths, low recognition in sports & lack of support for innovative minds.

Overall, the lack of good governance has impacted the lives of poor people for many years. For this, a desperate CHANGE was required - For the nation to prosper, the people needed empowerment.

Term 1 (2014) – Poll Promises

Shri. Narendra Modi in 2014 - I will make 3 promises in my individual capacity.

- **I will spare no effort to fulfill the party's promises**
- **I will not do anything for my personal gain**
- **I will not act out of ill will**

I was surprised when I read the election manifesto 2014 - Sabka Saath, Sabka Vikas.

There were **no freebies** to appease voters or some particular community. The initiatives & promises mentioned show that comprehensive groundwork was done to understand the nation & people's needs.

This book shares the election manifesto promises & delivered results.

1. Attend the Imminent

Promised

Price Rise

- Our immediate task will be to rein in inflation by several steps, such as:

- Put in place strict measures and special Courts to stop hoarding and black marketing.

- Setting up a Price Stabilization Fund.

- Unbundle FCI operations into procurement, storage, and distribution for greater efficiency.

- Leverage technology to disseminate Real-time data, especially to farmers - on production,

- prices, imports, stocks, and overall availability.

- Evolve a single 'National agriculture Market'.

- Promote and support area-specific crops and vegetables linked to the people's food habits.

Delivered

In 2013-2014, inflation was at a 6.4 % level, making food grains and food products very expensive.

Modi Govt. took many concrete measures to reduce inflation.

- 2019, the inflation was at 3.4%, down by 3 % in 5 years (2014-15, the inflation was 5.9%; in 2015-16, 4.9%; in 2016-17, 4.5%; in 2017-18, 3.6% and in 2018-19, 3.4 %

- In 2015-16, the Modi government set up a Price Stabilization Fund (PSF) that was used to procure agricultural produce at market prices.

- FCI and many State governments have developed their own Online Procurement Systems, which have brought transparency and convenience to the farmers through registration and monitoring of actual procurement.

- eNAM (Online National agriculture Market) was launched in 2016, providing farmers access to a nationwide market with prices commensurate with the quality of their produce - the platform to get at more reasonable prices.

- The year 2018 was celebrated as the "National Year of Millets."

Employment and Entrepreneurship

Promised

Under the broader economic revival, the BJP will accord high priority to job creation and opportunities for entrepreneurship. We will:

- Strategically develop high-impact domains like Labor-intensive manufacturing (viz. Textiles, footwear, electronics assembly, etc., and tourism.

- Strengthen the traditional employment bases of agriculture and allied industries, and retail -through modernization, as well as stronger credit and market linkages.

- Harness the opportunities provided by the upgradation of infrastructure and housing for its job-generating potential.

- Encourage and empower our youth for self-employment - incubating entrepreneurship as well as facilitating credit.

- Address the employability issue by initiating a multi-skills development program in mission mode. The focus will be on job creation and entrepreneurship in both rural and urban areas.

- Transform our Employment Exchanges into Career Centres - connecting our youth with job opportunities in a transparent and effective manner through the use of technology, as well as providing counseling and training.

Delivered

Prime Minister Narendra Modi's government launched various comprehensive schemes & initiatives to ensure key sectors were boosted & backed through constant engagement with respective sector ministries to bring many reforms to promote employment and entrepreneurship. Also, the government enabled channels of direct communication with key sector leaders/Unions to bring required development with changes to promote productivity and visibility.

- Schemes like the Focus Market Scheme, Market Linked Focus Product Scheme, and Focus Product Scheme Merchandise

Exports from India Scheme (MEIS). The Swadesh Darshan Scheme - theme-based tourist circuits, the Pilgrimage Rejuvenation and Spiritual, Heritage Augmentation Drive (PRASHAD), and "Destination Northeast" promoting tourism. Bharat's Tourism ranking improved from 65th place in 2014 to 40th place in 2018.

- The current Mahatma Gandhi National Rural Employment Guarantee Scheme (MGNREGS) was enhanced with an increase in budget from 33,000 Cr INR (2013-14) to 55,000 Cr INR (2018-19). Geo-tagging technology was introduced to bring more productivity and transparency and check monetary leakages. Prime Minister's Employment Generation Program (PMEGP) implemented by the Ministry of Micro, Small & Medium Enterprises, Pt. Deen Dayal Upadhyaya Grameen Kaushalya Yojana (DDU-GKY) scheme run by the Ministry of Rural Development, and Deendayal Antyodaya Yojana- National Urban Livelihoods Mission (DAY-NULM) implemented by the Ministry of Housing & Urban Affairs.

- The government has also implemented the National Career Service (NCS) Project, which comprises a digital portal that provides a nationwide online platform for jobseekers and employers for job matching in a dynamic, efficient, and responsive manner and has a repository of career content.

- More than 1,77,524 km of road construction was completed in rural areas (134 km/ day compared to 69 Km/day in 2014). Under the Housing for All scheme, more than 1.5 Cr houses were constructed for poor people across rural & urban.

- **Pradhan Mantri Mudra Yojana (PMMY)** is a scheme to extend collateral-free loans by Banks, Non-Banking Financial

Companies (NBFCs), and Micro Finance Institutions (MFIs) to small/micro business enterprises in the non-agricultural sector to individuals to enable them to set up or expand their business activities.

Standup India was launched to promote entrepreneurship amongst women, Scheduled Castes (SC) & Scheduled Tribes (ST) categories, to help them in starting a greenfield enterprise in manufacturing, services, or the trading sector and activities allied to agriculture. Banking loans from 10 lakhs to 1 Cr were extended. More than 54,000 loans were sanctioned to empower SC/ST & women entrepreneurs.

The Startup India scheme was introduced with the intent of cultivating startup culture and building a strong and inclusive ecosystem for innovation and entrepreneurship in India. For the first time in our Nation's history, more than 15900 startups were recognized under this scheme.

- In order to improve the employability of youth, around 22 Ministries/Departments introduced skill development schemes across various sectors.

Schemes like "SANKALP" and "Strive" were introduced for the skill development of youth in line with the needs of industry.

Enterprises creating new employment opportunities are being provided financial assistance under "PM Rojgar Protsahan Yojana."

More than 5 lakh youths benefited from the "National Apprenticeship Promotion Scheme."

Corruption

Promised

Corruption is a manifestation of poor governance. Moreover, it reflects the bad intentions of those sitting in power. All pervasive corruption under the Congress-led UPA has become a 'National Crisis.'

We will establish a system that eliminates the scope for corruption. We will do this through:

- public awareness

- Technology-enabled e-Governance - minimizing the discretion in the citizen-government interface.

- System-based, policy-driven governance - making it transparent.

- Rationalization and simplification of the tax regime - which is currently repulsive for honest taxpayers.

- Simplification of the processes and procedures at all levels - bestowing faith in the citizens, institutions, and establishments.

Delivered

Our Hon'ble Prime Minister Shri. Narendra Modi took significant measures not only to remove corruption but also to save the nation's money.

Key Schemes & Money Saved by Modi Govt:

Key Schemes	Money saved by Modi Govt
Direct Benefit Transfer (DBT)	Rs 1,85,000 Crore
Insolvency Bankruptcy Code (IBC)	Rs 1,10,000 Crore
Eliminate Fake / Duplicate Ration Cards	Rs 17,000 Crore
Reduce Health Care Expenses	Rs 16,000 Crore
LED Bulbs	Rs 50,000 Crore
Benami Property Law	Rs 6,000 Crore

- PM Modi himself led the initiative of bringing awareness to common people about the need for a corruption-free system & society for the development of the nation.

- Disbursement of welfare benefits directly to the citizens under various government schemes in a transparent manner through the Direct Benefit Transfer (DBT) initiative.

- Implementation of E-tendering in public procurements.

- Introduction of e-Governance and simplification of procedure and systems.

- Introduction of government procurement through the government e-Marketplace (GeM)

- Under PM Modi, Bharat was the government with the highest trust in Govt. with 85% (USA 51%, Russia 67%, Japan 57%)

Black Money

Promised

By minimizing the scope for corruption, we will ensure the minimization of the generation of black money. BJP is committed to initiating the process of tracking down and bringing back black money stashed in foreign banks and offshore accounts. We will set up a task force for this purpose and to recommend amendments to existing laws or enact new laws. The process of bringing back black money to India, what belongs to India, will be put in motion on priority. We will also proactively engage with foreign governments to facilitate information sharing on black money.

Delivered

Modi Govt has taken stringent steps to arrest the generation of black money as well as ensure that economic offenders are brought to book.

- Success of Demonetization

- Bharat's highest ever unearthing of black money, decisive blow to terrorism & naxalism, 2.24 lakhs of shell companies removed, increase in tax compliance, Digital payments getting a significant boost, increase in loan access & jobs for poor, cheaper loans for small & medium business and increased revenues to municipalities.

- As its first cabinet decision, it set up a court-monitored SIT, which had detected black money of more than **Rs. 70,000 crores**, including **Rs. 16,000 crores** in offshore accounts.

- In order to provide legal teeth to the fight against corruption, the Black Money (Undisclosed Foreign Income and Assets) and Imposition of Tax Act 2015 was enacted by the Modi government. The Act allows a penalty of up to 90% of the value of an undisclosed asset in addition to tax at 30%, as well as rigorous imprisonment in certain cases. These stringent penalties and imprisonment act as an effective deterrence against entities involved in stashing black money.

- Modi government has strengthened the Double Tax Avoidance Agreement (DTAA) with various countries, such as Mauritius, Singapore, Cyprus, etc. The government renegotiated tax treaties to curb treaty abuse, tax evasion, and round-tripping of funds—the practice of money stashed overseas by Indians returning home through tax haven countries. These amended tax treaties are considered a big victory in India's fight against black money.

- Under the leadership of PM Modi, the government has taken various proactive measures against black money stashed abroad, which have led to positive results. There has been a significant decrease in the loans and deposits in Swiss banks as well as in Swiss non-bank loans and deposits.

- The steps taken by the Modi government to check the flight of black money in offshore accounts include India and Switzerland signing a Joint Declaration on the introduction of the Automatic Exchange of Information (AEOI) on tax matters. This will ensure that India will receive information on accounts held by Indian residents in Switzerland from September 2019 for 2018 and subsequent years on an automatic basis.

- The Modi government successfully enacted the long pending Benami Transactions (Prohibition) Amendment Act, 2016 to enable the confiscation of Benami property and prosecution of Benamidar and the beneficial owner, which may result in rigorous imprisonment of up to 7 years and a fine of up to 2 percent of the fair market value of the property. The 24 dedicated Benami Prohibition Units (BPUs) have been set up all over India to ensure swift action in respect of Benami properties. This resulted in around 1,600 transactions being a part of provisional attachment while the value of properties under attachment is worth **Rs. 6,900 crores.**

- **The Fugitive Economic Offenders Act 2018 was introduced by the Modi government, empowering investigative agencies to go after absconding economic offenders. It allows law enforcement agencies to confiscate the assets of those who cheat the nation and flee the jurisdiction of Indian courts. This will force the accused to return to India and face trial for his offenses and, in turn, help the banks and financial institutions achieve higher recovery from financial defaults committed by fugitive economic offenders. Additionally, Fugitive Economic Offenders (Procedure for Conducting Search and Seizure), Rules, 2018 ensures faster attachment and confiscation of assets.**

- The anti-black money measures taken by the Modi Govt. have brought undisclosed income of about **1,30,000 Crore to tax**. Enforcing corporate accountability and accountability toward loans taken from public money is also an important way to clean the economy.

- From independence till 2008, that is, in 60 years, banks gave loans of Rs. 18 lakh crore. However, from 2008 to 2014, in just 6 years, the Congress government took this figure to Rs. 52 lakh crore. These created massive NPAs, which, too, were hidden by the UPA Govt.

Modi government not only unearthed these NPAs but also set about resolving them by passing the Insolvency and Bankruptcy Code. So far, the government has helped banks and creditors recover more than **Rs. 3 lakh crore**.

Decision and Policy Paralysis

Promised

The engine of government will be ignited again with strong willpower and commitment to public interest. We will also encourage the bureaucracy to make the right decisions and contribute their might to building a modern India.

Delivered

PM Modi is the only active Chief Minister to have taken over as Prime Minister, so he brings that rich 13 years (as Gujarat Chief Minister) of rich administrative experience which delivered good governance & was a great example across the nation.

- One of the first things that Modi did after he became Prime Minister was to hold a meeting with 77 secretaries of all government departments, where he encouraged them to work fearlessly and proactively. This was followed by extensive presentations that each department made directly to the PM. Cabinet notes had deadlines with a maximum 2 weeks time limit to reply to queries strictly imposed.

- Bharat's Act East policy empowered entire Northeastern states with better investment & infrastructure, linking the entire northeast with the rest of Bharat through a massive focus on developing the economy, agriculture, Tourism, roadways, railways & airports, delivered a transformational change across northeastern states.

- More than 1400+ obsolete laws were repealed.

- Modi Govt. introduces GST (One nation One Tax) – biggest tax reform in the nation.

- Bharat registered a new historic rise in Ease of doing business ranking (77th Rank in 2018 against 142nd in 2014)

Credibility Crisis

Promised

The BJP will work to restore the trust and credibility of the government. We will also ensure that the chain of responsibility and accountability is built into the system.

Delivered

Bharat has emerged as a self-assured and self-reliant nation that believes in working together for the collective well-being. Diplomacy, credibility, and leadership qualities of Prime Minister Shri Narendra Modi have transformed India's image on the international stage into an agenda-setter. Bharat has positioned itself on a global high table today. Our great nation's peace-loving nature & self-respect are being recognized and respected by the world.

- Out-of-box thinking, boldness of vision, and energetic execution which has reignited the 'Bharat Story.' In the process, India proved itself to be a major player in shaping evolving debates across issues, ranging from global governance reforms and climate change to transnational terrorism and cyber security.

- Path-breaking, Proactive, and Pragmatic – these 3 P's encapsulate the diplomatic initiatives and outreach of the Government of Bharat led by Prime Minister Narendra Modi

- Bharat diplomacy reinvigorated Bharat's ties with all P5 powers, with Prime Minister Narendra Modi visiting the US, China, France, Britain, and Russia, paving the way for marked acceleration of multi-faceted relations with all these countries. Bharat's multi-hued engagement with crucial regions of the world, including Africa, West Asia, Central Asia, and Southeast Asia, acquired a new vitality and a long-term vision, opening new vistas for mutually empowering cooperation.

- Bharat's Global Competitive Index ranking raised to 43rd place in 2019 compared to 60th rank in 2014.

2. Strengthen the Framework

Promised

Team India

Center-State Relations

We will place Center-State relations on an even keel through the process of consultation and strive for harmonious Center-State relations.

- Our government will be an enabler and facilitator in the rapid progress of states. We will evolve a model of national development, which is driven by the states. 2.

- Team India shall not be limited to the Prime Minister-led team sitting in Delhi but will also include Chief Ministers and other functionaries as equal partners.

- Ensure fiscal autonomy of states while urging financial discipline.

- Create 'Regional Councils of States' with common problems and concerns, with a view to seeking solutions that are applicable across a group of states.

- We will encourage cooperation among states on security-related issues and inter-state disputes, remove inter-regional economic disparities, and promote tourism.

- We recognize the special needs and unique problems of the hill and desert states. In consultation with the governments of these states, state-specific developmental priorities/ models will be evolved so that the aspirations of the people are met.

- Given the unique status of Union Territories (UTs), they will receive special attention. We will focus on developing and strengthening the economy of UTs. Tourism will be promoted, tribal welfare and their rights will receive full attention, and infrastructure and coastal area development will be given top priority.

- We reiterate our commitment to the protection and integrated development of our island territories.

- The moribund forums like 'National Development Council' and 'Inter-State Council' will be revived and made into active bodies.

- Involve the state governments in the promotion of foreign trade and commerce.

- Help the states mobilize resources through investments in industry, agriculture, and infrastructure.

Delivered

PM Modi, with his rich experience as Chief Minister, has stressed the need to leverage cooperative cooperative & competitive federalism to achieve all-around growth. Modi Govt's importance around governance reform has been the goal of building a more cooperative form of Center-state relations - PM Modi promised a new approach. Chief ministers worked together with the Center as a 'Team India' to resolve differences and achieve a jointly defined national interest.

- To empower states, the planning commission was removed & NITI Aayog was formed to further empower and strengthen the states. An important evolutionary change from the past will be replacing a Union-to-State one-way flow of policy with a genuine and continuing partnership with the states.

- The implementation of the Fourteenth Finance Commission recommendations increased the states' share of central taxation from 32 percent to 42 percent.

- Goods & Services Tax implementation - The GST revenue is shared between the Central and State governments in a ratio of 50:50 for most goods and services

- Modi Govt. has given states more fiscal responsibility with spending powers by giving them more untied funds.

- Policies were framed by seeking views from states first rather than asking states to adopt a centrally designed scheme. One example is the turnaround scheme for state-run power distribution companies, the Ujwal Discom Assurance Yojana.

- Modi Govt. has given states more fiscal responsibility with spending powers by giving them more untied funds.

- In a novel initiative, PM Modi was accompanied by 2 Chief Ministers on his visit to China. They participated in a landmark initiative: The Provincial Leaders Forum.

- In a major boost to the states, particularly the coal-rich states of East India, a major portion of the proceeds from the successful coal auctions would go to the states, helping them immensely.

- A Standing Committee of the Inter-State Council has been constituted for continuous consultation and processing of matters for the consideration of the Council.

Integrating the Nation – Its Vastness and Voices

Promised

All Indians living in different regions of the country have an equal stake in the progress of the country, and they have to be assured of the fruits of the progress.

Regional aspirations: BJP has always stood for greater decentralization through smaller states.

Northeast: Resource-rich Northeastern states are lagging behind in development due to poor governance, systemic corruption, and poor delivery of public services. NDA government had initiated. Concrete steps to address the issue of development of the Northeast by setting up the Ministry of Northeastern Region. We will empower this Ministry with a broader charter and non-lapsable funds for the rapid development of the region.

BJP will

- Put special emphasis on enhancing the connectivity within the region and to the rest of the country.

- There will be special emphasis on massive infrastructure development, especially along the Line of Actual Control in Arunachal Pradesh and Sikkim.

- Address the issue of flood control and river water management in Assam.

- Nurture more job-generating opportunities like tourism and the IT industry.

- Address the issue of infiltration and illegal immigrants in the Northeast region on a priority basis.

- This will include clear policy directions and effective control at the ground level.

- Complete all pending fencing work along the India-Bangladesh and India-Myanmar border, stepping up border security.

- Take measures for the safety of Northeastern students studying across the country, including setting up Hostels for Northeastern students at various educational centers.

- Deal with Insurgent groups with a firm hand.

- **Jammu and Kashmir**: Jammu and Kashmir was, is, and shall remain an integral part of the Union of India. The territorial integrity of India is inviolable. BJP will pursue an agenda of equal and rapid development in all 3 regions of the state - Jammu, Kashmir, and Ladakh.

- The return of Kashmiri Pandits to the land of their ancestors with full dignity, security, and assured livelihood will figure high on the BJP's agenda.

- The long pending problems and demands of refugees from Pakistan-Occupied Kashmir (POK) will be addressed.

- BJP reiterates its stand on Article 370, will discuss this with all stakeholders, and remains committed to the abrogation of this article.

- All steps will be taken to provide good governance, better infrastructure, educational opportunities, healthcare, and more job opportunities, leading to a better quality of life in the valley.

Seemandhra and Telangana: BJP is committed to doing full justice to Seemandhra and addressing the issues of development and governance of Seemandhra and Telangana.

Delivered

Northeast

PM Modi was the first PM to make the maximum number of visits to the Northeast States in his first 5 years. Modi wanted development across infrastructure, skills, connectivity, youth empowerment, agriculture & women empowerment. Prime Minister Narendra Modi considered the 8 Northeast states (Arunachal Pradesh, Assam, Manipur, Meghalaya, Mizoram, Nagaland, Sikkim, and Tripura.) as 'Ashta Lakshmi,' the 8 forms of the goddess of wealth, in the region. Modi Govt. focused on infrastructure development based on science and technology.

Development of the Northeast was seen as the heartbeat of Bharat's Act East Policy.

- Strengthening connectivity between Northeast and ASEAN via trade, culture, people-to-people contacts, and infrastructure. Bharat – Myanmar – Thailand trilateral highway.

- Inland waterways for transport of goods to important ports in ASEAN (19 new waterways).

- Northeastern Council has spent over Rs 2309 Cr in just three years on development in the region.

- No of projects increased from 56 to 138 in just 3 years.

- Comprehensive Scheme for power transmission and distribution systems for Northeast States (Rs 9865 Cr) approved by Modi Govt in 1st year of Modi Govt.

- 16 hydropower projects, installation of 694 MW of power generating capacity, 2540 km of transmission and distribution lines laid.

- 3840 km of national highways are sanctioned with an investment of Rs 32,600 Cr. In just 3 years, 1266 Kms of National Highways were constructed at a cost of Rs 13,500 Cr

- Rs 207 Cr was sanctioned to protect Majuli, the world's largest riverine island. Destination North is organized every year to showcase opportunities for business and tourism.

- First ever Northeast Investor's summit for Textiles to promote rich textile traditions of NE.

- Assam's National Register of Citizens, a supreme court-monitored exercise being conducted for the first time since 1951, is nearing completion. It is aimed at distinguishing Indian citizens living in Assam from undocumented migrants.

- 3,326 km of the sanctioned length of the border fence, 2746.44 km had been finished. The number of border posts has been increased, and more troops have been sent in.

- Govt. flagged off the Northeast Assistance Team of the Delhi Police. Hostels for Northeastern students in metropolitan cities were established.

- The Naga accord was signed in 2015 & Modi Govt. successfully concluded the dialogue on the Naga political issue, which has existed for 6 decades. It will advance a life of dignity, opportunity, and equity for the Naga people, based on their genius and consistent with the uniqueness of the Naga people and their culture and traditions.

Jammu and Kashmir (J&K)

PM Modi's special focus since 2014 ensured long-term progress and infrastructural development for J&K. Many developmental projects were successfully delivered to construct roads, bridges, tunnels, bunkers, dams, and educational institutions like AIIMS, medical and engineering colleges in Jammu and Kashmir. PM Modi has been working continuously over the last 5 years (2014-2019) to ensure the fruits of development reach everyone equally and continuously working with the mantra of 'Sabka Sath, Sabka Vikas.'

- 14 km long Zojila tunnel (Rs 6800 Crore) – Bharat's longest road tunnel and Asia's longest bi-directional tunnel. This tunnel will provide all-weather connectivity between Srinagar, Kargil, and Leh. It will cut down the time taken to cross the Zojila pass from the present 3 and a half hours to just 15 minutes.

- Two AIIMS institutes in Vijaypur (Jammu) and Awantipora (Srinagar) are transforming health care facilities, as well as health education and training in the state.

- The University of Ladakh - the first ever university set up in the Ladakh region of the state.

- One hundred percent electrification of households was achieved in Jammu and Kashmir under the central government's Saubhagya Scheme.

- 624-MW Kiru hydroelectric project in Kishtwar & W Dah hydroelectric project in Ladakh

- The 330 MW Kishanganga Hydropower Station, Pakul Dul Power Project & Jammu, Srinagar Ring Road.

- PM Modi initiated various dialogues with the Kashmiri Pandits community to understand their core needs & requirements in the areas of return, rehabilitation, and restitution. Modi Govt. worked on a blueprint to enable Kashmiri Pandits to live in a secure, smart, sustainable area within their homeland in the valley.

  Mastermind of Kashmiri Pandits genocide terrorist Yasin Malik was arrested by NIA.

- The Modi government, in January 2015, approved certain concessions for the refugees of Pakistan-Occupied Kashmir (PoK) - special recruitment drives for induction into paramilitary forces, equal employment opportunities in the state, admission for the children of refugees in Kendriya Vidyalayas. Modi Govt. always said that PoK and Gilgit-Baltistan are part of Jammu and Kashmir.

- A Rs 2,000-crore development package for displaced people of Pakistan-occupied Kashmir (PoK) living in the country was approved by the Modi Govt to provide financial support to 36,384 families.

Seemandhra and Telangana

Modi Govt. initiated multiple development projects for Seemandhra & Telangana progress. Continuous focus & funds were provided by various ministries to transform the states. PM Modi always showed special care and attention to the development of both states.

Seemandhra

While fulfilling its commitments under the Andhra Pradesh Reorganization Act 2014, the Modi Govt extended special assistance packages for Andhra development projects.

- Rs. 10169.20 crore, Rs. 20505.72 crore, and Rs. 19698.01 crore were transferred to the State of Andhra Pradesh under various heads from the Modi government in 2016-17, 2017-18, and 2018-19, respectively.

- The Polavaram Irrigation Project was declared a national project.

- Indian Institute of Petroleum & Energy was established in Visakhapatnam.

- National Institute of Information Technology in Kurnool.

- The Indian Institute of Science Education and Research has been established in Tirupati.

- The Indian Institute of Management has been established at Visakhapatnam.

- All India Institute of Medical Sciences was established in Guntur.

- A National Institute of Disaster Management is being established in the State of Andhra Pradesh.

- Expansion of Visakhapatnam airport & New terminal for Tirupati airport

- The National Highway Authority of India has taken several steps for the establishment of the National Highways in the State of Andhra Pradesh.

- Railways implemented many measures to establish rapid rail and road connectivity between the newly proposed capital of Andhra Pradesh and Hyderabad and other cities in the region.

Telangana

Modi government is committed to the development of Telangana. Under the 13th Finance Commission, Telangana got Rs 16,597 crore, which was increased to a whopping Rs. 1,15,900 crore under the Modi government in the 14th Finance Commission.

Implemented infrastructure projects worth 30,000 Cr

The Modi Govt. has released states' share of union taxes, according to which Telangana received ₹9,745.4 crores in 2014-15, ₹12,350.72 crores (2015-16), ₹14,876.61 crores (2016-17), ₹16,420.06 crores (2017-18), ₹18,560.88 crores (2018-19).

In terms of grants, the Modi Govt. released ₹2,128 crores in 2014-15 through XIII Finance Commission awards and ₹1,546 crores (2015-16), ₹1,991.84 crores (2016-17), ₹1,225.95 crores (2017-18), ₹1,806.13 crores (2018-19).

Decentralization and People's Participation

Promised

BJP has stood for greater decentralization through devolving of powers to the states. A vast reservoir of **People's Power** has not yet been tested in the real sense. BJP to involve the people in governance as functionaries and facilitators.

- **People's Participation**: Our developmental process will be a people's movement - of Jan Bhandari. We will make them the active drivers of development rather than mere passive recipients.

- **People's Engagement**: Through Proactive, Pro-People Good Governance, we will ensure the government itself directly reaches out to the people, especially the weak and marginalized sections of society.

- **We will further evolve the Public-Private Partnership (PPP) model into a People-Public-Private Partnership (PPPP) model.**

- **BJP is committed to strengthening self-governance at the local level, and we will empower Panchayati Raj Institutions with extensive devolution of the 3 Fs - Functions, Functionaries, and Funds.**

- Good performers among the Panchayats will be rewarded with additional developmental grants.

- Strengthen the institution of the **Gram Sabha**, respecting their inputs and initiatives for the development process.

- We will actively involve people in **policy formulation** and **evaluation** through various platforms.

- We will encourage **Openness** in the government, involving all stakeholders in the decision-making processes.

Delivered

People's Participation (Swachh Bharat Mission)

A clean India would be the best tribute India could pay to Mahatma Gandhi on his 150th birthday anniversary in 2019," said Shri Narendra Modi as he launched the Swachh Bharat Mission at Rajpath in New Delhi. On 2 October 2014, the Swachh Bharat Mission was launched throughout the length and breadth of the country as a national movement.

As per the World Health Organization, the Swachh Bharat Mission saved 3 lakh children.

People's Engagement

Digital India – A program that transformed India into a digitally empowered society and knowledge economy. The program is centered on 3 key vision areas, namely digital infrastructure as a core utility to every citizen, governance, and services on demand, and digital empowerment of citizens.

Digital India is transformational in nature and successfully delivers central Government services to citizens electronically.

Benefits

- UN e-governance index India ranks at 96th (2018); up by 28 places since 2012 (124th place in 2012)

- E-Governance services to common people per day increased from 64.4 Lakhs (2013) to more than 9 Cr per day (Aug 2018)

- Aadhaar – Digital Identity & good governance covered for 120 Cr people (61 Cr in 2013)

- Connected 1,09,900 Gram panchayats (as of May 2018) through digital network connectivity, empowering rural people digitally.

- Lakhs Common Services Centres (CSC) – a center to deliver major government services; created digital entrepreneurs across small towns & villages. 10 Lakhs jobs created with 54,000 women working at CSC.

- Digital Literacy for villages – 6 Crore rural people targeted to gain digital knowledge within 2 years,

- Digital Health Care – Connecting 232 hospitals under e-Hospitals to serve common people for various health care services (3.3 Cr patients covered so far)

- Skill Development in Electronics Systems & design Manufacturing (2.8 Lakhs students trained so far)

- 2.4 Cr senior citizen (Jan 2019) pensioners benefited through Digital Life Certificate, thus avoiding their physical presence to receive the pension amount.

People-Public-Private Partnership (PPPP) Model

When we make people part of the policy formulation and also make partners in execution, the people assume ownership of the project and hence will leave no stone unturned to make the program successful.

PM Modi transformed the PPP model to make development a mass movement by empowering people & harnessing their potential for the success of the government's efforts.

PM Modi's glorious initiatives of people's participation and public partnership across sectors like housing, health, education, and physical infrastructure delivered the vision and courage of proactive PM Modi, who not only designed proactive and pro-people policies but also decentralized power to administrative machinery in partnership with public and people at large.

3 Fs - Functions, Functionaries, and Funds

As per the 2011 census, nearly 70% of Bharat is rural; attainment of Sustainable Development Goals at the national level will require actions at the grassroots of villages—that is, at the Panchayat level.

PM Modi believed funds and functions must be transferred to empower rural local bodies for their holistic growth and to achieve national development.

Bharat to be a developed country - it is necessary that along with the cities, rural India should also be developed and strengthened in capacity-building, education, and technical efficiency. PM Modi empowered Panchayati Raj Institutions (PRIs) since they are the backbone of a successful and good governance system for any country.

Modi Govt has awarded Rs. 200,292.2 crores to Panchayats for 2015-2020 (as per the 14th Finance Commission), which is more than 3 times the grant of the 13th Finance Commission.

Saansad Adarsh Gram Yojana (SAGY) was launched in Oct 2014, and each Member of Parliament adopted a Gram Panchayat and guided its holistic progress, giving importance to social development at par with infrastructure. By involving villagers and leveraging scientific tools, a Village Development Plan is prepared under the leadership of a Member of Parliament.

21 Schemes have been amended by various Ministries / Departments of the government of India to give priority to SAGY Gram Panchayat projects.

3. Reform the System

Promised

India First

BJP believes in India being one country, one people, and one nation. BJP recognizes the importance of diversity in Indian society and the strength and vibrancy it adds to the nation. The party believes in the principle of unity in diversity.

Delivered

From day 1, the Modi Govt. always believed in & delivered Nation First. Always First. The Govt. wants to make people conscious and capable; empowering every person in the country was the main goal of the Modi Govt.

PM Modi was committed to the very idea of nation-building, the foundation of which was laid in 2014. While fulfilling the basic needs of countrymen, the Govt. also moved forward toward realizing its aspirations of building a Strong, Safe, Prosperous, and all-inclusive Bharat.

Bharat became the fastest-growing economy in the world. Low inflation, the fiscal deficit under control, foreign exchange reserves growing, and the impact of Make in India are clearly visible.

The Nation First initiatives delivered significant results across the following segments.

- Development for All

- Infrastructure for new Bharat

- Putting Farmers First

- Accelerating growth

- Speed & Scale of Transformation

- Eliminating Corruption

- Harnessing Yuva Shakti

- World Sees a new Bharat

- Building a healthy Bharat

Open Government and Accountable Administration

Promised

- Administrative reforms will be a priority for the BJP. Hence, we propose to implement them through an appropriate body under the PMO.

- The following specific action will be initiated:

- Digitization of government records will be taken up as a top priority so that they are easily accessible.

- Performance review and social and environmental audits would be mandated for all government schemes and programs.

- Open up the government to draw expertise from the industry, academia, and society into the services.

- Government will be redefined by elimination of whatever is obsolete in laws, regulations, administrative structures, and practices and would be purposive.

- We will generate 'Kartavya Bhavna' among public servants as people's lives and productivity are dependent on the quality and efficiency of public services.

On the whole, the hallmarks of our governance model would be:

- People-centric
- Policy-driven
- Time-bound delivery
- Minimum government, maximum governance

Delivered

To deliver effective & efficient governance, one needs commitment, dedication & willingness to deliver time-bound results. Modi Govt. created a strong blueprint to comprehensively cover the "Accountability & open Govt Model" from the beginning itself.

Digital India - A program to make Bharat into a digitally empowered society and knowledge economy. Bharat, in the 21st Century, must strive to meet the aspirations of its citizens where government and its services reach the doorsteps of citizens and contribute toward a long-lasting positive impact.

The Digital India Program successfully transformed Bharat into a digitally empowered society and knowledge economy by leveraging IT as a growth engine of the new Bharat.

Prime Minister Narendra Modi regularly interacted with district magistrates (DMs), taking direct feedback about the progress and status of the implementation of various government schemes and programs. The interaction helped to review the performance and ascertain the challenges that are being faced by various departments in the districts in a mission mode in convergence with all stakeholders.

Digital India delivered digital empowerment to citizens:

- Universal digital literacy.

- All digital resources are universally accessible.

- All government documents/ certificates are available on the Cloud.

- Availability of digital resources/services in Bharat languages.

- Collaborative digital platforms for participative governance.

- Portability of all entitlements for individuals through the Cloud

The Digital India Program successfully transformed Bharat into a digitally empowered society and knowledge economy by leveraging IT as a growth engine of the new Bharat.

More than 1400 obsolete laws were removed to enable a corruption-free environment, smooth administration & timely services to common citizens.

E-Governance: Easy, Efficient and Effective

Promised

Bharat is the IT capital of the whole world. But back home, the benefits of IT have not percolated down. This will be a high priority area for the BJP, as IT touches the lives of ordinary men and women.

BJP will:

- Focus on increasing the penetration and usage of broadband across the country. Deployment of broadband in every village would be a thrust area.

- Leverage technology for e-governance and engage proactively with the people through social media for participative governance and effective public grievance redressal mechanism.

- Generate IT-based jobs in rural and semi-urban areas.

- Make technology-enabled products affordable for students.

- Use technology to reduce the burden of books on children. Make all institutions and schools e-enabled in a phased manner. Digital learning and training are to be used extensively.

- Pursue a mission mode project under the 'National Rural Internet and Technology Mission' for the use of telemedicine and mobile healthcare for rural healthcare delivery; use of IT for agriculture for real-time information; Self Help Groups; retail trade and SMEs; and rural entrepreneurs, etc.

- Initiate a National e-Governance Plan to cover every government office from the center to the panchayats. The 'E-Gram, Vishwa Gram' Scheme in Gujarat is to be implemented nationwide.

- Promote e-Bhasha - National Mission for the promotion of IT in Indian Languages.

- Focus on bringing SC/ST, OBCs, and other weaker sections of society within the ambit of IT.

- enabled development.

- Deploy IT to protect India's priceless cultural and artistic heritage, which includes digitization of all archives and museology.

- Promote 'open source' and 'open standard' software.

- Mandate digitization of all government work to reduce corruption and delays.

- Set up High-speed digital highways to unite the nation.

- Use technology to reduce Transmission and distribution losses.

- Use mobile and e-banking to ensure financial inclusion.

Delivered

Modi Govt. believes, follows & delivers e-Governance as the channel through which poor & common people can get government services &receive benefits directly, thus eliminating the corruption from middlemen.

Benefits of e-Governance

- UN e-Governance index ranks India at 96th (2018), up by 28 places since 2012 (124th place in 2012)

- E-Governance services to common people per day increased from 64.4 Lakhs (2013) to more than 9 Cr per day (Aug 2018)

- Aadhaar – Digital Identity & good governance covered for 120 Cr people (61 Cr in 2013)

- Connected 1,09,900 Gram panchayats (as of May 2018) through digital network connectivity, empowering rural people digitally.

- 2.92 Lakhs Common Services Centres (CSC) – a center to deliver major government services; created digital entrepreneurs across small towns & villages.

- 10 Lakhs jobs created with 54,000 women working at CSC.

- Digital Literacy for villages - 6 Crore rural people targeted to gain digital knowledge within 2 years.

- Digital Health Care – Connecting 232 hospitals under e-Hospitals to serve common people for various health care services (3.3 Cr patients covered till Aug 2018).

- Broadband connectivity increased from 6.1 Crore (2014) to 41.2 Crore (2018).

- Optical fiber cable coverage increased from 7 lakh Km (2014) to 14 lakh Km (2018).

- Internet coverage increased from 25.1 Crore (2014) to 44.6 Crore (2018).

- Ujwal DISCOM Assurance Yojana or UDAY Scheme - The largest contributor in Bharat's power reforms for the turnaround of state distribution entities. A total of 27 states and UTs have joined this scheme for financial and operational turnaround.

- UDAY scheme has yielded savings of nearly Rs 12,000 Crores to the state power distribution companies (2018). Significantly, Bharat has turned around from a net importer of electricity to a net exporter of electricity, exporting around 5,798 Million Units to Nepal, Bangladesh, and Myanmar in 2017.

Institutional Reform – Administrative, Judicial, Police and Electoral

Promised

Administrative

- The administration and its members will be made truly accountable to their tasks as well as the people through a rigorous evaluation process.

- Good performance will be rewarded; non-performers will be given opportunities and training support to improve.

- Rationalization and convergence among the Ministries, departments, and other arms of the government will be ensured to focus on delivery.

- Open up government to draw expertise from the industry, academia, and society.

- Services of youth, in particular, will be tapped to contribute to governance with Fellowship and Internship programs launched at various levels.

Delivered

- Modi government has provided an incorruptible administration at the helm. PM Modi gave a specific focus on accountability and the delivery of effective good governance.

- As a measure of good governance, the Modi Govt. made online filing of performance appraisals mandatory for IAS officers.

- Launched Central Govt. employees Online app to enable Govt. employees to stay updated on a real-time basis with postings & appointments at the senior level.

- Abolition of affidavit & verification by Gazetted officer is replaced by self-attestation to reduce time and effort on the part of citizens as well as the officials in government officers.

- For the first time in the history of the Indian Administrative Service (IAS), the new batch of Officers of the IAS were posted as Assistant Secretaries in the Central Secretariat for a period of 3 months.

- In a first-of-its-kind initiative, the Modi Govt. opened jobs across various government departments like editorial writers, researchers, data scientists, software developers, video editors, social media experts, graphic designers, and app developers for professionals working in the private sector.

KV Kamath – Ex-ICICI Bank and Ex-Infosys – BRICS Bank Chairman

Kris Gopalakrishnan – Ex-Infosys – Digital India

Arvind Panagariya – Professor of Economics at Columbia University – Vice-Chairman NITI Aayog

- A National Scheme of Apprenticeship Training started.

- On 2 Aug 2014, the HRD ministry rolled out a special internship program with the involvement of young talent to get a fresh perspective on the formulation of policies, implementation of projects, and various initiatives in the education sector.

- On-going internship programs in the Ministry of External Affairs, Finance Ministry, and Ministry of Corporate Affairs.

- Modi Govt. hiked the fellowships for RA/SRF/JRF by around 50%.

Judicial

Promised

- Give high priority to judicial reforms to address the issue of the appointment of judges, filling the vacancies, opening new courts, and setting up a mechanism for speedy clearance of the backlog of cases at various levels in the judiciary.

- Initiate a mission mode project for filling the vacancies in the judiciary and for doubling the number of courts and judges in the subordinate judiciary.

- Set up a National Judicial Commission for the appointment of judges in higher judiciary.

- Create a fund for the modernization of courts to improve their operational efficiency.

- Reform the criminal justice system to make the dispensation of justice simpler, quicker, and more effective after examining the recommendations of the earlier reports on this subject.

- Initiate the computerization and networking of courts all over the country.

- Expand alternative dispute redressal mechanisms through Lok Adalats and Tribunals.

- Implement the National Litigation Policy in letter and spirit to reduce the average pendency time of cases.

- Periodically review and refine/ scrap outdated laws.

- Set up a comprehensive National e-Library, empowering Lawyers.

- Aim to enhance the number of women in the Bar as well as Bench, reducing the gender gap in the judiciary.

- Develop India into a Global Hub for Arbitration and Legal Process Outsourcing.

- BJP will simultaneously reform the legal system to make it more accessible to the common man.

- Make legal information open and freely accessible.

- Run legal awareness programs and introduce them in the school curriculum - making the common man aware of his rights and duties.

Delivered

- Modi Govt. commitment to bring transformation in the judicial system is commendable, with many initiatives introduced to bring "Justice for all" through the empowerment of transparent processes & technological strength in high courts increased from 906 (2014) to 1079 (201,8), helping to resolve pending cases.

- Strengthened judicial infrastructure - Increase of 34% in additional court halls since 2014

- Exclusive Fastrack courts for a speedy trial of offenses against SC, ST, women & senior citizens (from 281 in 2014 to 727 in 2018)

- Tele-law-services – Online free legal advisory for poor people (18,900+ persons, 6000+ women, 8000+ SC, ST & OBCs benefited under this initiative)

- 1428+ obsolete laws removed in just 3 years.

- The settlement of cases in Lok Adalats increased (the number of cases settled in Lok Adalat increased from 66.06 lakh during 2011-13 to 1.36 crore in 2014-16.).

- The draft national litigation policy under formulation to make the government a responsible and efficient litigant.

- The eCourts Mission Project Phase II was implemented (2015-19) with Rs. 1078 crores & Computerization of 16,089 district and subordinate courts has been completed.

- The National Judicial Data Grid (NJDG) for district & subordinate courts has been created as an online platform that now provides information relating to judicial proceedings/decisions (10 Crore cases & 7 Crore orders & judgments available on portal https://ecourts.gov.in)

- National Digital Library was launched in June 2018 (<u>https://ecourts.gov.in/ecourts_home/</u>) with 1.7 Crore **content from** more than 160 sources, and 30 lakh users are registered.

Police

Promised

We will work with the states to empower them with the authority, independence, and resources necessary to deliver:

- Roll out a comprehensive strategy for bringing the Indian Police to par with international standards.

- Facilitate training and capacity-building of Police forces.

- Modernize the police force, equipping them with the latest technology.

- Initiate the networking of police stations across the country for intelligence sharing and crime control.

- Strengthen Investigations, making them Swift, Transparent, Fair, Clear, and Decisive - acting as an inescapable deterrent to wrong-doers and a protective shield to the innocent.

- Modernize our prison system with technology and infrastructure to strengthen security, human rights, and correctional dimensions.

- Train and technologically enable the police to track, pursue, and prevent cybercrime.

- Bring Coastal states together on a common platform to discuss issues of Marine Policing.

- Give special emphasis to improving the working conditions and welfare of police personnel.

Delivered

Modi Govt. discharges numerous responsibilities, the important among them being - internal security, border management, center-state relations, administration of Union Territories, management of Central Armed Police Forces, disaster management, etc. Modernization of the police force was the top priority of the Modi Govt. Several initiatives & programs were launched to empower the nation's police force to protect our people every day & every hour.

- The government launched single digit pan-India emergency phone number, '112', under the Emergency Response Support System (ERSS)

- Launch of Crime and Criminal Tracking Network & Systems (CCTNS) – Online platform services providing a smooth interface between citizens and police

- Govt. launched 2 separate portals to strengthen Women Safety - Cyber Crime Prevention against Women and Children (CCPWC) portal to check objectionable online content and the National Database on Sexual Offenders (NDSO) to aid in monitoring & investigation of sexual crimes (https://cybercrime.gov.in)

- In order to recognize the dedicated efforts of the CAPF personnel and encourage high standards of professionalism, Govt. announced the institution of 5 Police Medals. - the Home Minister's Special Operation Medal, Antarik Suraksha Medal, Asadharan Aashuchan Padak, and Utkrisht & Ati-Utkrisht Seva Medal.

- Union Home Minister's Medal for Excellence in Police Investigation" to promote high professional standards of

Investigation of Crime in the State/UT Police and Central Investigating Agencies in the country.

- Prime Minister Shri Narendra Modi dedicated the National Police Memorial to the nation. This Police Memorial represents all State/UT Police Forces and Central Police Organizations of the country. Since 1947, 34,844 police personnel have been martyred.

- Govt. supporting the states/UTs in implementing the E-Prisons project that aims to introduce efficiency in prison management through digitization - The availability of prisoner's details on an electronic platform will be useful to track the status of prisoners and smooth functioning of the prison system.

- The government has adopted a well-coordinated Coastal Security Policy and has worked to secure the country's coasts through an integrated approach (15,000 km long land border and 7,516 km long sea border,1,382 islands, 3,337 coastal villages, 11 major ports, 241 non-major ports, and 135 establishments including those of space, defense, atomic energy, petroleum, shipping, etc.)

- Govt approved setting up of National Coastal Police Academy to train 3000 coastal police personnel every year.

Electoral

Promised

BJP is committed to initiating electoral reforms to eliminate criminals.

- To evolve a method of holding Assembly and Lok Sabha elections simultaneously

- Reducing election expenses for both political parties and the government will ensure certain stability for State governments. We will also look at revising expenditure limits realistically.

Delivered

- Modi Govt. initiated the idea of 'one nation, one poll,' synchronizing assembly and Lok Sabha elections. However, this requires a constitutional amendment, for which there is no consensus among the political parties at present. The Law Commission of India released a draft report on Simultaneous Elections in 2018. The Standing Committee on Personnel, Public Grievances, Law and Justice also submitted a report on the "Feasibility of Holding Simultaneous Elections to House of People (Lok Sabha) and State Legislative Assemblies" in 2015

- **The scheme of Electoral Bond was introduced in The Finance Bill, 2017 during <u>Union Budget 2017-18</u> when the maximum limit of cash donation to political parties was capped at ₹2,000**

Widen The Platform Poor and Marginalized – Bridge the Gap

Promised

Our government will be a government of the poor, marginalized, and left behind. The Bharat of tomorrow will have 125 crore such dreams and will be built on the same. We will not only empower our citizens with the ability to dream, we will enable them with the capability to actualize their dreams.

- Strengthen the Delivery of poverty alleviation programs through convergence, transparency, and efficiency.

- Identify the 100 most backward districts of the country to bring them at par with other districts through prioritized and integrated development.

- Strengthen the people's natural resource base to tide over natural calamities.

- Aim to gainfully employ rural poor in agriculture and allied activities.

- Enable the urban poor to develop skills so that they can take advantage of emerging opportunities.

Food Security

Review the successful PDS models and incorporate the best practices to revise the existing PDS for the benefit of the common man

- Address the issue of under-nutrition and malnutrition

- Encourage the production of cereals, pulses, and oils

- Radically transform the Food Corporation of India (FCI)

- Ensure contingency stocks for any exigencies arising due to natural calamities or external factors

- **Seek the participation of voluntary organizations in running community kitchens**

Delivered

On May 20, 2014, PM-elect Narendra Modi gave a historic speech in the Central Hall of Parliament. "NDA government would be a government of the poor, by the poor, and for the poor. In short, the NDA government would be dedicated to the poor." Prime Minister Narendra Modi believed that the country's economic resources should be utilized for the poor's well-being through good Governance.

The Modi government has ensured that citizens, irrespective of their caste, religion, gender, region, economic class, or political preferences, receive the benefits they are entitled to. The government's efforts to extend welfare provisioning and poverty alleviation have received recognition from global institutions like the IMF, crediting the Modi government for ending extr**eme** poverty in the country. Modi Govt. lifted 5 Cr (50 Million) people out of poverty in just 4 years through its people welfare schemes.

- PM Bank account opening scheme (Jan Dhan), PM Housing Scheme (Awas), PM Family Healthcare Scheme (Ayushman Bharat), PM LPG Gas Connection Scheme (Ujjwala Yojana), toilets construction under Swachh Bharat, PM Small business loans scheme (Mudra), PM Accident & Life Insurance Scheme (Suraksha Bima & Jeevan Jyoti Bima), PM Farmers Crop Insurance Scheme (Fasal Bima yojana) & Soil Health card Scheme.

Scheme	Target People	Beneficiaries
Bank account opening	Poor People	33 Cr (330 million)
Accident & Life Insurance	Common People	20 Cr (200 million)
Soil Health Card	Poor Farmers	18 Cr (180 million)
Small Business loan	Common People	15 Cr (150 million)
Crop Insurance	Poor Farmers	14 Cr (140 million)
Free toilet construction	Poor Women	9.7 Cr (97 million)
Free Gas connection	Poor Women	6.4 Cr (64 million)
Housing scheme	Poor Women	1.5 Cr (15 million)
Free Healthcare	Poor People	10 Lakhs (1 million)

- PM Modi launched the Aspirational Districts Program (ADP) to quickly and effectively transform 112 of the most under-developed districts across the country. The ranking is based on the incremental progress made across 49 Key Performance

Indicators (KPIs) under 5 broad socio-economic themes - Health & Nutrition, Education, Agriculture & Water Resources, Financial Inclusion & Skill Development, and Infrastructure. (championsofchange.gov.in)

- PM Modi inaugurated the Asian Ministerial Conference on Disaster Risk Reduction (AMCDRR) 2016 & signed a statement of cooperation with the United Nations. Various governmental and non-governmental organizations such as the Indian Space Research Organization (ISRO), Defense Research and Development Organization (DRDO), Coal India Ltd., National Disaster Response Force (NDRF), GSDMA (Gujarat State Disaster Management Authority), Oil and Natural Gas Corporation (ONGC), Indian Red Cross Society displayed their initiatives in disaster risk reduction, mitigation, preparedness and response. Govt. inaugurated the International Workshop on Disaster-Resilient Infrastructure (IWDRI) in 2018.

- Govt approved the continuation of the Prime Minister's Employment Generation Program (PMEGP) beyond the 12th Plan for three years from 2017-18 to 2019-20, with a total outlay of Rs.5,500 crore. The government also continued the Mahatma Gandhi National Rural Employment Guarantee Scheme.

- The government launched the Skill India scheme, which enabled and mobilized many Indian youth to take up skill training, become employable, and earn their livelihood. Eight thousand 4 hundred sixty-one training centers, 2249 training partners & more than 5 Lakh youths received job placements under this scheme.

Food Security

- Govt launched the Poshan Abhiyan scheme – a first-of-its-kind initiative to tackle malnutrition through multimodal interventions. Targeted to reduce malnutrition through convergence, use of technology & a targeted approach. Rs 2122 Cr funded (2017-18,2018-19) benefiting 10 Cr people.

- PM Modi approved the Umbrella Scheme "Green Revolution – Krishonnati Yojana" in the agriculture sector. The Umbrella Scheme comprises 11 Schemes/Missions with Rs 33 269 Cr. These schemes helped to develop the agriculture and allied sectors in a holistic and scientific manner to increase farmers' incomes by enhancing production and productivity and achieving better returns on produce.

- **Construction of Godowns**: A total storage capacity of 22.23 lakh MT has been added in just 4 years under the PEG Scheme.

- **Silos** - Use of modern technology in storage: A road map for the creation of 100 Lakh MT storage capacity in the form of Steel Silos by FCI and other agencies, including State governments on PPP mode for wheat and rice was approved & construction of 6.25 Lakh MT Steel Silos have been completed.

- **Online Procurement Management System (OPMS)**: FCI has developed software for OPMS, which is being used for procurement in the KMS 2016-17. So far, 17 out of 19 major procuring states have fully implemented OPMS.

- **Depot Online system**: To bring all operations of FCI Godowns online to check leakages and automate operations at the depot level, a "Depot Online" system was launched. The Depot Online System is being successfully run in **530** FCI depots and 156 CWC depots.

SCs, STs, OBCs, and Other Weaker Sections- Social Justice and Empowerment

Promised

The BJP is committed to bridging the divide following the principle of social justice (Samajik Nyay) and social harmony (Samajik Samrasata)

- A high priority for SC, ST, OBCs, and other weaker sections would be to create an ecosystem for education and entrepreneurship.

- BJP is committed to the eradication of untouchability at all levels.

- BJP is committed to eliminating manual scavenging.

- BJP will look at more effective ways to pull these people out of the poverty line.

- BJP will ensure that the funds allocated for schemes and programs for SC, ST, OBCs, and other weaker sections are utilized properly.

- A mission mode project would be made for housing, education, health, and skills development.

- A special focus would be on the children, especially the girl child, with regard to health, education, and skill development.

  BJP will initiate a 'Vanbandhu Kalyan Yojna' at the national level to be overseen by a 'Tribal Development Authority.' This scheme will focus on:

- Setting up the entire education network for tribals.

- Upgrading housing, water, and health facilities.

- Electrification of tribal hamlets and provision of all-weather roads.

- Initiating new economic activities

- Promoting the products associated with the tribal culture by setting tribal haats in tourist towns and other centers.

- Ensure that the tribal land is not alienated.

- Facilitating access to minor forest produce and creating a network of rural haats (markets). "Establishing the National Centre for Tribal Research and Culture to preserve the tribal culture and languages.

- Enhancing the funds for tribal welfare and development

Delivered

PM Modi always followed & believed in the path of Dr. Babasaheb Ambedkar to deliver sustaining social justice and social inclusion for the SC/ST communities. For the first time in the history of independent Bharat, many social transformation schemes & initiatives were delivered, empowering women, farmers & youth of SC/ST communities.

- A historic 95,000 Cr INR was budgeted for the welfare of SC/ST communities (2018-19). Unprecedented rise of 41% increase in OBC community budget allocation (2018-19).

- National Fellowship for SC (NFSC) – Rate increased to 31,000 INR & 35,000 INR (Junior & Senior)

- Free coaching for SC and OBC students (increased income eligibility from 4.5 Lakhs to 6 lakhs)

- SC/ST student stipend was raised (from 1500 INR to 2500 INR – for local students) & (from 3000 INR to 5000 INR for outstation students)

- Substantial increase in pre-metric & post metric scholarship (SC & OBC students)

- Standup India scheme – loan up to 1 Cr INR for SC/ST women entrepreneurship

- Mudra Scheme – 50% of beneficiaries were SC/ST women (7 Cr)

- For the first time, the Modi Govt. developed places associated with the life of Dr. Babasaheb Ambedkar.

- New path-breaking legislative amendments & establishment of an exclusive special court for speedy trial of offenses against SC/ST

- Schemes like Jhan Dhan (Bank account opening), free housing, free toilet construction, free Gas connection, and Direct Benefit Transfer empowered the SC/ST communities, especially women & girl children.

- The Scheme "Vanbandhu Kalyan Yojana (VKY)" was launched by the Ministry of Tribal Affairs in 2014 Tribal Affairs with an initial allocation of Rs. 100.00 Crore INR for 10 State's Tribal development. Rs 200 Crore INR was released in 2015-16 for 21 states.

Minorities – Equal Opportunities

Promised

- Ensure that the young, and the girl child in particular, get education and jobs without discrimination.

- Strengthen and modernize minority educational systems and institutions, dovetailing them with modern requirements. National Madrasa modernization program would be initiated.

- Empower with vibrancy in Livelihood and Entrepreneurial opportunities.

- Augment their traditional artisanship and entrepreneurial skills, which are the backbone of our cottage and small-scale industry - strengthening these sectors through better market linkages, branding, and access to credit.

- Empower Waqf Boards in consultation with religious leaders, taking steps to remove encroachments from and unauthorized occupation of Waqf properties.

- Curate their rich heritage and culture - maintenance and restoration of heritage sites; digitization of archives; preservation and promotion of Urdu.

- Ensure a peaceful and secure environment where there is no place for either the perpetrators or exploiters of fear.

- Facilitate the setting up of a permanent interfaith consultative mechanism to promote harmony and trust under the auspices of religious leaders.

Delivered

PM Modi believed every citizen of this great nation, Bharat, has every right to get development & empowerment, including minorities. He initiated several programs & schemes which benefited minority communities.

Modi Mission - Education is an effective step toward empowerment. The government led by Prime Minister Shri Narendra Modi successfully moved forward toward educational and social empowerment of all weaker and backward sections of the society. Ministry of Minority Affairs has worked with commitment to "3E- Education, Employment & Empowerment".

Thousands of educational institutions of all minority communities, including Madarsas, have been included in the mainstream education system by connecting them with "3T-Teacher, Tiffin, Toilet."

- Scholarships have been provided to more than 3 crore 11 lakh students belonging to Minority communities, which includes 60% female students.

- The school dropout rate among Muslim girls, which was earlier more than 70 percent, has now been reduced to about 40 percent due to awareness and educational empowerment programs of the government.

- More than 31,305 Cr INR was spent on various educational empowerment schemes for minorities in just 3 years (2016-17, 2017-18, 2018-19)

- More than 1003 Cr INR was spent on various economic empowerment schemes for minorities in just 3 years (2016-17, 2017-18, 2018-19)

- More than 3435 Cr INR was spent on various infrastructure development schemes (PMJVK) for minorities in just 3 years (2016-17, 2017-18, 2018-19)

- More than 5 lakh 43 thousand youths have been provided employment and employment opportunities through job-oriented skill development schemes.

- More than 2 lakh artisans have been provided employment and employment opportunities in national as well as international markets through "Hunar Haat."

- Haj pilgrimage has been made 100 percent digital/online. For the first time, about 1300 Muslim women from India went to Haj without "Mehram" (male companion). Separate accommodation and transport were arranged for these women Haj pilgrims in Saudi Arabia

- Qaumi Wakf Boards taraqquiti Scheme (QWBTS), under which financial assistance is provided to State Waqf Boards (SWBs) toward computerization and digitization of Waqf records (84% waqf properties already digitized)

- Modi Govt. held regular review meetings with all delegations from Muslims, Christians, Buddhists, Parsis, Sikhs & Jains, reflecting a commitment to protect all constitutional institutions, democratic values, and religious rights of all sections moving forward with "inclusive growth."

Neo-Middle Class – Meet Their Aspirations

Promised

- Educational scholarships and educational facilities.

- Medical insurance and quality healthcare services.

- Middle-income housing.

- Efficient public transport systems

Delivered

The middle class, which accounts for one-third of the population, is a powerful force in realizing Bharat's dreams of prosperity and development. The middle class is becoming a beacon of change in all aspects of life in a rapidly changing Bharat, contributing toward nation development, system stability, great courage, and better decision-making ability.

Modi government has also left no stone unturned in order to give middle class dreams wings. Keeping in mind the importance of the middle class in Bharat's resolve to become a developed nation, PM Modi is making continuous efforts to make it a development partner. The middle class has also been given special priority, ensuring that a new Bharat emerges, scaling new heights.

- National Scholarship Portal – (1.4 Cr students benefited)

- PM Atal Innovation Mission – (5441 Schools benefited)

- 16 Indian Institutes of Technology (IIT) in the country before 2014; Modi Government has started 7 new IITs in the last 5 years.

- 9 Indian Institute of Information Technology (IIITs) before 2014; the Modi government has started 15 new IIITs.

- 13 Indian Institute of Management before 2014; Modi Government has started 7 new IIMs in the last 5 years.

- 7 All India Institute of Medical Sciences level institutes; Modi Government has started/approved 15 new AIIMS in the last 5 years.

- PM Modi introduced the National Healthy Policy 2017, the Mental Healthcare Act, and the Allied & Healthcare Professionals Bill 2018 to build a healthy Bharat.

- PM Heart stent scheme - Life-saving coronary stents have been capped at Rs 28,000, which is a cost drop of about 85% from commercially available.

- PM Knee surgery scheme - Knee implant prices have been capped at Rs 54,720, which is a cost drop of about 70% from commercially available.

- World's cheapest & most affordable accident & life Insurance – 12 Rs INR per year/person (accident insurance) & 330 Rs INR per year/person (Life Insurance) (Total 20 Cr people benefited).

- The Real Estate Regulatory Authority (RERA) Act 2016 provides protection to home buyers. Protecting middle class investment in housing: After RERA, builders pay interest and compensation for delays.

- More than 1.53 Cr affordable houses were constructed under the PM housing scheme (Awas Yojana).

- National Aviation Policy 2016 transformed the sector, with more people traveling by air than by AC trains.

- UDAN Scheme – Affordable Air travel (total 103 operational airports since independence)

- Bharat's metro network has risen to 18 cities from 5 in 2014.

Rural Areas – High Priority

Promised

A full-fledged program for 'Rural Rejuvenation' will be made and implemented, which will comprise integrated strategies for the personal, economic, and social well-being of the villagers. Through the idea of Rurban, we will bring urban amenities to our rural areas while retaining the soul of the village.

Major thrust areas for rural development would be to improve village-level infrastructure in terms of roads, potable water, education, health, supply chain, electricity, broadband, job creation, security in rural areas, and linkage to markets.

Delivered

Under the vision of Prime Minister Narendra Modi, the government is committed to the cause of rural development and farmers' progress. Rural Innovation and Rural Bharat will play a crucial role in developing the new Bharat. The government focused on the sustainable and inclusive growth of rural Bharat by increasing livelihood opportunities, providing social safety, and developing rural infrastructure. The 5 major rural development themes:

Rural Housing (through Pradhan Mantri Awaas Yojana – Gramin)

Rural Employment (through Mahatma Gandhi National Rural Employment Guarantee Scheme)

Rural Connectivity (through Pradhan Mantri Gram Sadak Yojana)

Rural Livelihood (through Deendayal Antyodaya Yojana – National Rural Livelihoods Mission)

Rural Skilling (through Deen Dayal Upadhyaya Grameen Kaushalya Yojana and Rural Self-Employment Training Institutes)

- More than 11 Cr rural people benefited from 100 days of guaranteed employment.

- More than 91 Lakhs houses are sanctioned under the "Rural Housing for All" Scheme.

- 9.91 Cr toilets constructed in rural households.

- 3.18 lakhs Common Services Center (for Govt Services)

- 1.21 Lakhs Gram Panchayats connected by optical fiber.

- 5.54 Lakhs people across rural areas trained under Rural Skill Development

- 1.69 Lakh km of road construction was completed in rural areas (134 km/ day compared to 69 Km/day in 2014).

- 18,600 villages electrified (100% household electrification)

- Bank account for Rural/Semi-urban areas (Jhan Dhan Scheme) – a total of 20 Cr people benefited.

- 96 Lakhs houses constructed under PM rural housing scheme (PMAY-Gramin)

- eNAM – Online National agriculture Market for farmers (585 markets, 16 states, 2 UTs added under this scheme)

- Modi Govt. launched Shyama Prasad Mukherji Rurban Mission (SPMRM) in 2015, with an outlay of Rs. 5142.08 crores INR.

Urban Areas – High Growth Centers

Promised

Urban areas should become symbols of efficiency, speed, and scale.

- Major steps will be undertaken in Transport and Housing for 'Urban Upliftment' in Bharat.

- We will initiate building 100 new cities equipped with the latest in technology and infrastructure - adhering to concepts like sustainability, walking to work, etc.- and focused on specialized domains.

- The approach to urban development will be based on integrated habitat development - building on concepts like Twin cities and Satellite towns.

- Upgrade existing urban centers, transitioning focus from basic infrastructure to public utility services Waste and Water Management - for clean and healthy city life.

- Cleanliness and sanitation will be given priority, and efficient waste and water management systems will be set up. Model towns will be identified for rolling out integrated waste management infrastructure. Wi-Fi facilities will be made available in public places and commercial centers.

- Urban poverty alleviation scheme would be a key thrust area.

- Use technology for scientific, strategic, and long-term town planning - including GIS-based mapping. Build quality integrated Public Transport systems, discouraging usage of private vehicles.

Delivered

Urban cities contribute nearly 65 percent of the country's GDP and 90 percent of tax revenue.

Modi government has embarked on the most comprehensive and ambitious planned urbanization program undertaken anywhere in the world. One of the most significant new developments that took place is the embracing of urbanization." The government is investing and spending more in cities than has ever been done in this country.

The Missions of Pradhan Mantri Awas Yojana (Urban), Atal Mission for Rejuvenation, and Urban Transformation & Smart City Mission are not only transforming the country's urban landscape but also ensuring ease of living for the citizens. As compared to the overall investment of Rs 1.57 lakh crore during 2004-14, the investment in Urban rejuvenation during

2014-19 is Rs 10.31 lakh crore, which translates into a 554% increase. The investment in PMAY(U), AMRUT & SCM is about Rs. 8 lakh crore.

- Bharat's metro network has risen to 18 cities from 5 in 2014

- National Aviation Policy 2016 transformed the sector, with more people traveling by air than by AC trains.

- More than 1.53 Cr affordable houses were constructed under the PM housing scheme (Awas Yojana)

- Ten lakh families benefited from the PMAY-U credit-linked subsidy scheme (CLSS). The middle-income group families with income up to 18 lakh per annum are being funded for houses for the first time.

- Smart City Mission - One of the most transformational urban missions launched in 2015 for the development of 100 cities. Two thousand 7 hundred ninety-three projects worth Rs. 88,89 Cr are completed.

- Atal Mission for Rejuvenation and Urban Transformation (AMRUT) was launched on 25th June 2015 in selected 500 cities and towns across Bharat. The Mission focused on the development of basic infrastructure in the selected cities and towns in the sectors of water supply, sewerage and septage management, stormwater drainage, green spaces and parks, and non-motorized urban transport. More than 22 Crores of the urban population have benefited from these initiatives.

- To move from water scarcity to water security, 1,132 projects worth Rs 33,900 Cr are under implementation (2019)

- For Recycle & reuse of wastewater, 622 sewerage & septage management projects worth Rs. 26,589 Cr are under implementation.

- 37 Lakh sewer connections have been provided, while another 108 Lakh sewer connections will be provided.

- To recreate green spaces for a healthy lifestyle, 1,048 parks costing Rs 593 Cr have been developed. 1,356 Parks costing Rs 1,004 Cr are under development. These are equipped with women, children, and Divyang-friendly features.

- Deen Dayal Antyodaya Yojana – National Urban Livelihoods Mission (DAY-NULM) was launched by Modi Govt to reduce poverty and vulnerability of urban poor households on a sustainable basis. Also, it enhances employment opportunities and incomes of the urban poor.

- DAY-NULM scheme will benefit the urban poor in 1,505 new towns in the North, 991 towns in the South, 375 in the West, 249 in the East, and 130 more towns in the Northeast.

- Under DAY-NULM, 2.47 Lakhs Self Help Groups (SHGs) received revolving funds, 4.72 lakhs candidates got jobs, 3.84 lakhs persons given micro-enterprise loans, 1126 shelters made operational.

- Over 13 lakh houses are being built using new technologies. Online Building Permission Systems (OBPS), which has been implemented in 1,705 ULBs, including all ULBs in 11 states/ UTs, is ensuring ease of living for the citizens.

Leap Forward: Social Security – A Caring Government, Passionate Society

Children – the Future of the Nation

Promised

BJP will take the following steps to ensure the survival, development, participation, and protection of children:

- Lay special emphasis on vulnerable children, especially those belonging to vulnerable communities like SCs, STs, OBCs, migrants, slum dwellers, street dwellers, and those with disabilities. Ensure effective implementation of the Right to Education and Right to Food Security Act.

- Review, amend, and strengthen the Child and Adolescent Labor (Prohibition and Regulation) Act, 2012, and the Integrated Child Protection Scheme (ICPS).

- Focused efforts will be made to address the issue of anemia.

- Reduce the burden of books on children without compromising on the quality of education.

- **Endeavor to inculcate values among children.**

Delivered

Children are the future of our nation. The well-being of children is essential for a country's development as they constitute the future human resource of the country.

PM Modi delivered on mission mode, ensuring the development, care, and protection of children through cross-cutting policies and programs, spreading awareness about their rights, and facilitating access to learning, nutrition, and institutional and legislative support to enable them to grow and develop to their full potential.

- The Samagra Shiksha scheme - an integrated scheme for school education from pre-school to class XII

- Free coaching for SC and OBC students (increased income eligibility from 4.5 Lakhs to 6 lakhs)

- SC/ST student stipend raised (from 1500 INR to 2500 INR – for local students) & (from 3000 INR to 5000 INR for outstation students)

- Substantial increase in pre-metric & post metric scholarship (SC & OBC students)

- Modi Govt. approved amendments to the Child and Adolescent Labor Act of 2012 in May 2015. The proposed changes included a prohibition of all children below 14 years of age

- In 2018, PM Modi launched the Anemia Mukt Bharat (AMB) strategy to reduce the prevalence of anemia in six population groups - Children (6-59 months), Children (5-9 years), Adolescents girls and boys (10-19 years), Pregnant women, Lactating women and Women of Reproductive Age (WRA) group (15-49 years) in life cycle approach through life cycle approach.

- No homework for students of classes I and II and the prescribed weight limit of school bags for each class are part of the fresh directives issued by the Modi Govt. to states and Union Territories across the country.

- The National Council of Educational Research and Training (NCERT) recommended only 2 books (Language and Mathematics) for classes I & II and 3 books for Classes III to V (Language, Environmental Studies, and Mathematics). NCERT has also made available all their textbooks for free access through the web (pathshala.nic.in) and mobile devices.

- Pareeksha pe Charcha – PM Modi's interactive session with students across the country was launched in 2018.

Senior Citizens

Promised

- Provide financial support, exploring ideas like additional tax benefits and higher interest rates.

- Invest in setting up and improving old-age homes.

- Harness their experience in the National Interest.

- Devise schemes and programs to engage senior citizens as volunteers/part-time workers in various government development programs in urban and rural areas.

Delivered

PM government implemented various schemes and programs to provide senior citizens with a healthy, happy, empowered, dignified, and self-reliant life, along with strong social and inter-generational bonding.

The government is aware of the need for love, care, medical, housing, etc., of the senior citizens. For this purpose, various schemes/programs are being implemented by the Modi government for the welfare of senior citizens.

- The exemption of interest income on deposits with banks and post offices is to be increased from Rs. 10,000 to Rs. 50,000. TDS is not required to be deducted under section 194A.

- Pradhan Mantri Vaya Vandana Yojana (PMVVY) - The scheme enables old-age income security for senior citizens through the provision of assured pension/return linked to the subscription amount based on government guarantee to Life Insurance Corporation of India (LIC)

- The Senior Citizen Welfare Fund (SCWF), launched in 2016, is a fund that provides financial support to the Below Poverty Line (BPL) category senior citizens. It was introduced by the Modi government to help senior citizens who do not have any means of livelihood.

- Modi government set up MyGov, a web portal that connects the people to the government and provides a platform for them to participate in democracy. This portal is acceptable to all of us, irrespective of age.

Specially Abled

Promised

- Enact the 'Rights of the Persons with Disabilities Bill' (RPWD).

- Use technology to deliver low-cost, quality education to specially abled students in-home through e-learning.

- Identify each and every special needs person across the country - establishing a web-based disability registration system to issue universal ID for all applicable government benefits (healthcare, transportation, jobs, education, etc).

- Ensure disabled-friendly access to public facilities, public buildings, and transport.

- Ensure maximum economic independence of the disabled by creating more income generation models for them.

- Support and aid voluntary organizations working for the care of the disabled.

- Provide a higher tax relief for the family member taking care of the disabled.

Delivered

Under the leadership of Prime Minister Modi Ji in 2014, the issues related to persons with Disabilities have been put at the forefront of government initiatives. Prime Minister, with a view to changing social attitudes and recognizing the potential within them, addressed them as "Divyangjan." Accordingly, this department was also renamed the "Department of Empowerment of Persons with Disabilities (DEPWD)."

- Under the provision of section 40 of the RPwD Act 2016, the Modi government formulated rules for persons with disabilities, laying down the standards of accessibility for the physical environment, transportation, information, and communication (from 7 to 21 categories).

- PM Modi launched Samagra Shiksha – an integrated scheme for School Education covering children with special needs from classes I to XII.

- Launched the Unique Disability ID (UDID) Project in 2016-17 with the objective of creating a national database for Persons with Disabilities (PwDs) and issuing UDID cards for all disabilities.

- In the year 2018-19, an outlay of Rs.102 Cr has been supported toward Child With Special Needs (CWSN) grants.

- The scholarship scheme was launched in 2014 to pursue a scholarship in technical education. Rs 30,000 toward tuition fees & Rs 20,000 as contingency allowance

- 917 identified websites of State Govt/UTs will be accessible through ERNET India

- Indian Sign Language Research And Training Center was established in 2015

- 650 railway stations & 1000 Govt buildings provided with accessibility features for persons with disabilities.

- All 34 International & 48 domestic airports have been provided with accessible features.

- Special camps were organized for the distribution of aids & assistive devices to 12 lakh persons with disabilities worth Rs 700 Cr.

- Reservation in government jobs for Persons with Disabilities increased from 3% to 4%

- Deendayal Disabled Rehabilitation Scheme (DDRS) - 516 Projects supported by DDRS running in 27 states/UTs and 348 districts.

Youth – Making India Unstoppable

Promised

- We will initiate the 'Young Leaders program' in all sectors to recognize, reward, and involve these exceptionally talented youth to serve as role models and mentors for others.

- Set up the National Youth Advisory Council.

- BJP will initiate a nationwide 'district level incubation and accelerator program' to encourage innovation and entrepreneurship.

- The procedure to avail of student loans will be simplified, and loans will be made affordable.

- Set up neighborhood Children's/ Youth Parliament across India that leads to vibrant student committees.

- Will launch a program, 'Youth for Development."

Delivered

PM Modi believed the 21st century belonged to Bharat, and the youth of our great nation had the potential to change the world's structure. Today, Bharat is one of the fastest-growing economies in the world, and the youth in the country is the major catalyst for this growth. The nation has confidence and expectations in our youth to take the country forward and facilitate it.

- The National Young Leaders Program (NYLP) was launched in December 2014. The scheme had 5 components.

  Neighborhood Youth Parliament: To develop the platform of youth clubs of NYKS (Nehru Yuva Kendra Sangathan) in the shape of a vibrant 'neighborhood youth parliament' to educate the youth club members about contemporary socio-economic development issues and to involve them in debate/ discussions on such issues.

  Youth for Development Program: To channel the immense youth energy toward nation-building by involving them in Shramadaan (voluntary labor) on a large scale all over the country.

National Young Leaders Awards: To motivate the youth to strive for excellence in their respective fields by recognizing and rewarding the outstanding work done by them.

National Youth Advisory Council: To seek active involvement of the youth leaders as well as other stakeholders in the decision-making process on youth-related issues.

National Youth Development Fund: To mobilize funds for youth development from non-government sources like CSR funds.

- PM Modi launched the "Skill India' scheme – 13,000 training centers opened across Bharat for 1 Cr youths to achieve training.

- The "Startup India" scheme was launched for talented youth entrepreneurs who wanted to start their own businesses. More than 15,900 startups are recognized under this scheme.

- Atal Innovation Mission Scheme - Promotion of an ecosystem of innovation and entrepreneurship at various levels - higher secondary schools, science, engineering, and higher academic institutions, and SME/MSME industry, corporate and NGO levels. 2400 Atal Tinkering Lab created.

Promotion of Sports

Promised

- BJP will promote all sports - traditional and modern.
- More funds will be allocated to sports, and we will encourage the state governments to discharge their responsibility fully in the promotion of sports.

- Steps would be taken to inculcate a culture of sports at the school level by arranging sports facilities and training needs to promote a healthy lifestyle and make sports a compulsory part of the school curriculum.

- Launch a 'National Sports Talent Search System' so that extraordinary sporting talent can be identified at a very young age. Such promising boys and girls will be selected for special training. The existing rural sports program and National Women's Sports Festival will be broadened to reach every village and to identify talent for nurturing and excellence development.

- An attractive career path needs to be planned for sportspersons, providing career security through jobs in government, PSUs, and the private sector.

- Establish sports academies across the country.

- A special scheme would be devised for sportspersons to ensure social security.

- Encourage business houses to patronize sports and sportspersons.

- **Mandate all new housing colonies to include sports facilities.**

Delivered

PM Modi gave the utmost priority to Sports. Sport is an integral part of the nation-building process, as it plays an important role in terms of individual development, community development, social inclusiveness, and economic development. One of the most important factors that enable a nation to become a sporting power is the identification and development of the right talent.

- In the 2018 budget, the Modi Govt allocated a total of Rs 2196.36 crore for the sports ministry, compared to 1938.16 crore in 2017

- Modi Govt. called upon corporate houses to spend a portion of their CSR funds toward the promotion of sports. In 2014, Rs. 53.36 Crores were spent on 'encouraging sports' under CSR. That increased to Rs. 134.76 crores in 2015

- In March 2017, the government announced that it would provide pensions to former Indian international medal-winning sportspersons. In February 2018, the government announced a double pension for meritorious sportspersons under the scheme 'Sports Fund for Pension to Meritorious Sportspersons.'

- The National Sports Talent Search Portal was launched in 2018 - a kind of initiative to identify the best talent & provide a level playing field to all the applicants, and create a competitive environment (www.nationalsportstalenthunt.in)

- Khelo India Scheme – A mass movement to promote the culture of sports & fitness among youth. Annual assistance of Rs 5 Lakhs per year for 8 years to talented players

- The first Khleo India School Games launched in Jan 2018 (3507 participants from 27 states/7 UTs). Rs 1756 Cr allocated for 2017-18 to 2019-20.

- 1178 players availed of a scholarship program under the Khelo India Talent Identification Development scheme with 6.28 Lakhs given to residential players & additional 1.2 Lakhs Out of Pocket Allowance (OPA) transferred directly to bank accounts

- National Sports University (Manipur) was approved in 2018

- Pandit Deendayal Upadhyay National Welfare Fund for Sportspersons (PDUNWFS) aims to assist outstanding sportspersons of the past, living in indigent circumstances, who had brought glory to the country in sports.

- **Bharat recorded its best-ever performance (2018) in the Gold Coast Commonwealth Games with 66 Medals, Jakarta Asian Games with 69 Medals, and Para Asian Games with 72 Medals.**

Women – The Nation Builder

Promised

- Women's welfare and development will be accorded a high priority at all levels within the government, and the BJP is committed to 33% reservation in parliamentary and state assemblies through a constitutional amendment.

- Launch a national campaign for saving the girl child and educating her - Beti Bachao - Beti Padhao. Structure a comprehensive scheme, incorporating best practices from past successes like Balika Samruddhi, Ladli Laxmi, and Chiranjeevi Yojana to support and encourage positive attitudes among families toward the girl child.

- Program for women's healthcare in a mission mode, especially focusing on domains of Nutrition and Pregnancy - with emphasis on rural, SCs, STs, and OBCs.

- We will enable women with training and skills - setting up dedicated Women ITIs and Women wings in other ITIs.

- Strict implementation of laws related to women, particularly those related to rape.

- Fund for relief and rehabilitation of rape victims lies unused at the Center as the government has not worked out the modalities of dispensation. BJP will clear this on priority.

- The government will create an Acid Attack victims welfare fund to take care of the medical costs related to treatment and cosmetic reconstructive surgeries of such victims.

- Make police stations women-friendly and increase the number of women in police at different levels.

- Using information technology for women's safety.

- Set up an All Women Mobile Bank to cater to women.

- Special skills training and business incubator park for women.

- Setting up a special business facilitation center for women.

- Expand and improve upon the network of women / working women hostels.

- Set up a dedicated W-SME (Women Small and Medium Enterprises) cluster in every district.

- Review the working conditions and enhance the remuneration of Anganwadi workers.

- Special adult literacy initiatives would be started for women with a focus on SCs, STs, OBCs, and slum residents.

- We will ensure that the loans to Women Self Help Groups are available at low-interest rates.

- Special programs aimed at girls below the poverty line, tribals, and indigent women.

- Appropriate measures would be taken to check female foeticide, dowry, child marriage, trafficking, sexual harassment, rape, and family violence.

- We will transform the quality of life of women in Rural India by providing electricity, tap water, cleaner fuel, and toilets in every home.

Delivered

As per census 2011, 48.5% of our population are women. If a woman is empowered, a nation gets empowered. Women play a vital role in uplifting not only the family but also the nation.

Hon'ble PM Modi believed that a "women empowerment & women-led development" based nation can only transform. Many women's welfare schemes were launched to empower women. For the first time in history, India is the first country to implement so many welfare schemes for women's empowerment in the world.

- Women (Reservation in Services) Bill 2016 was introduced in Rajya Sabha - to provide for the reservation of posts and appointments for women in services under the central government. Many discussions were initiated by the government to take forward the formalization of the women's reservation bill.

- The Beti Bachao, Beti Padhao (BBBP) Scheme was launched by Prime Minister Narendra Modi on January 22, 2015. The key elements of the scheme include the Enforcement of Pre-Conception & Pre-Natal Diagnostic Techniques (PC & PNDT) Act, nationwide awareness and advocacy campaign, and multi-sectoral action. There is a strong emphasis on mindset change through training, sensitization, awareness-raising, and community mobilization on the ground. The scheme was launched initially in 100 districts & later expanded to all 640 districts (census 2011) with Rs 208 Cr allocated (2015-2018).

- Under-5 Child Mortality (Female) has reduced from 45 in 2014 to 36 in 2018.

- Percentage of First Trimester ANC Registration has shown improvement from 51% in 2014- 15 to 71% in 2019.

- PM Surakshit Matritva Abhiyan (PMSMA) Scheme – Launched to ensure good health of mother & child (More than 14641 health Center benefiting 1.8 Cr poor pregnant women.

- Mission Indradhanush was launched to vaccinate pregnant women & children (more than 87 lakhs pregnant women benefited).

- Maternity Benefit Act 2017 – paid maternity leave extended to 26 weeks – highest in the world.

- Poshan Abhiyan – First-of-its-kind initiative to tackle malnutrition through multi-modal intervention.

- Tough laws enabled by Govt – Provision of the death penalty for rape of girl child below the age of 12. The minimum punishment for rape of a girl under 16 years increased from 10 years to 20 years.

- A compensation scheme for Women Victims/Survivors of Sexual Assault and other crimes was launched in 2018. It covers a number of offenses, including rape, acid attack, harassment, domestic violence, etc.

- A compensation scheme for women victims/survivors of sexual assault/other crimes in 2018 was introduced.

- Women made up 15 % of the police force in India between 2015 and 2016, going from around 123,000 to over 140.000.

- The government launched the Himmat app to ensure women's safety & dignity.

- More than Rs 6700 Cr with 26 projects recommended under Nirbhaya Fund.

- The Bharatiya Mahila Bank (BMB) was launched in 2014 & later merged with the SBI on 1 April 2017

- **Skill India Mission**, a mega drive initiated by the Modi Govt, has transformed the lives of over 35.56 Lakh women through skill training, empowering them for better and secured livelihoods.

- They added more than 54 working women hostels & approved the addition of 190 hotels to accommodate 19,000 working women.

- Mudra Scheme – 70% are women beneficiaries (10 Cr +)

- Anti – Trafficking bill passed in Lok Sabha – Stringent penalties for crime against women.

- Self Help Groups increased 5 times from 5 Lakh SHGs covering 52 lakh families (2014) to 20 lakh SHGs covering 2.25 Cr families in just 4 years (Rashtriya Gramin Ajivika Mission).

- Swachh Bharat Mission – More than 9.7 Cr toilets constructed across the country (Sanitation coverage increased from 38% in 2014 to 98% in 2019).

- PM Housing Scheme (PMAY), women beneficiaries were given priority in house allocation under this scheme.

- More than 7 Cr free LPG connections given to poor women under UJJWALA yojana.

- 18,600 villages electrified.

Education – Enroll and Excel

School Education

Promised

- NDA's flagship program 'Sarva Shiksha Abhiyan': Mechanism, would be set up for its performance audit and to have real-time information about its performance.

- Universalization of secondary school education and skills development through functional school shall be seriously pursued with a particular focus on rural, tribal, and difficult areas.

- Girls shall be provided with all possible help to continue and complete their school education.

- The digital divide shall not be allowed to create further divisions in children's learning situations.

- Special pedagogy would be developed for differently-abled students.

- On priority, a national modernization program for madrasas would be started.

- Mid-day meal schemes would be revitalized in terms of management and delivery.

- We will explore ways to reduce the daily burden of carrying books to school for children, which would also entail the use of technology for education as a mission mode project.

- Establish a national E-Library to empower school teachers and students.

- Initiate a multi-country student exchange program to broaden the horizon of school-going children.

- The creative talents of students will be recognized and encouraged.

Delivered

Prime Minister Narendra Modi emphasizes the transformative potential of education in shaping the nation's future. PM Modi always highlights education's crucial role in propelling the country toward its goals & acknowledges the significance that education holds the key to altering the destiny of Bharat. Many missions were initiated & delivered big changes in the education system & impacted lakhs of children & youth across the nation.

- The web portal 'ShaGun' was launched for the Sarva Shiksha Abhiyan. 'Online Monitoring' captures **the progress** of the scheme as states, schools, and teachers enter information in real-time. The 'Repository' is documentation of best practices and reports on the scheme.

- Modi government launched Samagra Shiksha - An Integrated Scheme for school education, w.e.f. 2018-19 extending from pre-school to class XII.

- Beti Bachao Beti Padhao was launched in 2015. This scheme addressed the issues of declining Child Sex Ratio (CSR) and enabling girl child education.

- Over 1000 scholarships available per annum

- Modi Govt. implemented an Umbrella Scheme for Providing Education to Madarsas/Minorities (SPEMM) – Rs 120 Cr allocated (2016-17, 2017-18) benefiting more than 32,000 madrasa teachers.

- The government has adopted an elaborate monitoring mechanism at Central, State, and District levels to ensure quality food is served to children as well as utilization of funds under the Scheme.

- No homework for students of classes I and II and prescribed weight limit of school bags for each class are part of the fresh directives issued by the Modi Govt. to states and Union Territories across the country.

- The National Digital Library (NDL) was launched in 2018 (more than 1.9 Cr e-books with more than 200+ languages)

- Under the Rashtriya Yuva Sashaktikaran Karyakram (RYSK) scheme, the government enabled international youth exchange programs with various countries to develop an international perspective among the youth.

- Atal Tinkering Labs launched to empower innovative mindsets in school children – 5441 schools covered.

Higher and Professional Education

Promised

- Enhancing the pivotal role of the teachers by reworking the work culture of teacher training institutions with a goal to prepare committed and performing teachers.

- A mechanism for close interaction between industry (including SME), academia, and community would be instituted.

- A needs assessment exercise will be done to identify the future needs across sectors, and the same will be used to develop appropriate courses for higher education to ensure that the country has adequate manpower for every sector, both established and emerging, in the economy.

- It will provide autonomy with steps to ensure accountability for institutions of higher learning.

- It will raise the standard of education and research so that Indian universities become at par with the top global universities and find their place in the global league.

- UGC will be restructured, and it will be transformed into a Higher Education Commission rather than just being a grant distribution agency.

- We will revisit the Apprenticeship Act to facilitate our youth's earnings while they learn.

Delivered

- 'Prashikshak' - a teacher education portal, was launched with a vision to strengthen District Institutes of Education and Training (DIETs) and bring quality teachers into the Indian school education system.

- Pandit Madan Mohan Malaviya's National Mission on Teachers and Teaching (PMMMNMTT) scheme was launched in December 2014 to address the issues of the supply of qualified teachers and attracting talent into the teaching profession.

- Global Initiative of Academic Networks (GIAN) – An initiative launched in November 2015 to garner the best international knowledge and experience in the country's higher education so as to enable Indian students & faculty to interact with the best academic and industry experts from across the world.

- The government has constituted a Committee to draft the National Education Policy **(NEP)** under the Chairmanship of eminent scientist Dr. K. Kasturirangan.

- The government granted autonomy to 76 Educational Institutions, including 62 universities (5 Central universities, 21 State universities, 34 Deemed universities, and 2 Private universities) and 14 Colleges across the Country.

- PM Modi launched many programs such as IMPRINT India, Uchhatar Avishkar Yojana (UAY), Global Initiative of Academic Networks (GIAN), Scheme for Transformational & Advanced Research in Fundamental Sciences (STARS), Scheme for Promotion of Academic & Research Collaboration (SPARC), Impactful Policy Research in Social Science (IMPRESS) to promote research in India.

- PM's Research Fellowship (PMRF) - aimed at attracting the talent pool of the country to doctoral (Ph.D.) programs of Indian Institutes of Technology (IITs) and Indian Institute of Science (IISc) for carrying out research in cutting-edge science and technology domains, with focus on national priorities.

- The government approves the draft act for setting up the Higher Education Commission of India Bill 2018 by repealing the UGC Act.

- Govt. passed The Apprentices (Amendment) Bill 2014 to enable establishments to set up apprenticeship programs faster and those which are more effective for the industry.

Vocational Training

Promised

- Would set up Massive Open Online Courses (MOOC) and virtual classrooms to make it convenient for working-class people and housewives to further their knowledge and qualifications.

- Correspondence courses will be started in new domains for self-employment, family-run businesses, entrepreneurship, and innovation, and these courses will be provided for free to women.

- BJP will set up a National Commission on Education to report in 2 years on the state of education and the reforms needed. Based on the report, the BJP will implement a National Education Policy.

Delivered

- "Study Webs of Active Learning for Young Aspiring Minds" (SWAYAM) scheme was launched in 2016, providing an integrated platform and portal for Massive Open Online Courses(MOOCs) with more than 1000+ courses.

- Govt approved UGC (Online Courses) Regulations, 2018, as a landmark reform in the field of Higher Education. Higher Educational Institutions can offer Certificate, Diploma, and Degree Programmes in full-fledged online mode in line with their regular programs.

- The government constituted a Committee to draft the National Education Policy under the Chairmanship of eminent scientist Dr. K. Kasturirangan & submitted the report in 2018

Skills – Focusing on Productivity and Employability

Promised

- Skill Mapping - to help scientifically plan our national human resource development that India would need (like engineers, architects, doctors, nurses, lawyers, accountants, plumbers, carpenters, welders, etc.).

- Launch a 'National Multi-skill Mission'

- We will run short-term courses in the evenings, focusing on employable skills.

- We will also set up Centers of Excellence in various sectors in partnership with the industry.

- To ensure industry-responsive manpower, we will bring together industry, universities, and

- government.

- We will promote vocational training on a massive scale. Rigid segregation of formal education and skill development will be broken; a mechanism will be established to give vocational qualifications of Academic Equivalence.

- We will also create institutional mechanisms to refresh and upgrade abilities through continuing education - to make them employable.

- Put emphasis on imparting soft skills to enhance employability, including a national program on foreign languages.

- Launch a national program for digital empowerment through computer literacy of the people, especially the youth.

- We will assess the talent and capacity of our youth from an early age so they can be groomed accordingly.

- We will push for greater practical and research training, encouraging real-world experience through internships and apprenticeships.

Delivered

Prime Minister Modi emphasized the need to provide this youthful manpower with the skills and ability to tackle global challenges.

If the 20th century saw Bharat's foremost technical institutes – the IITs – make a name for themselves globally, the 21st century required that India's ITIs (Industrial Training Institutes) acquire global recognition for producing quality skilled manpower

Our Prime Minister believes that Bharat can become the world's largest provider of skilled workforce. In order to prepare for this, there is a need to map manpower requirements, not just in Bharat but globally as well.

- The National Skill Development Mission (NSDM) was launched by PM Modir in 2015 to create convergence across sectors and states in terms of skill training activities.

- Over 25000 training centers opened across Bharat training in 633 trades & 1 Cr youngsters trained with 20 ministries enrolled in Skill Development schemes.

- Pradhan Mantri Kaushal Vikas Yojana (PMKVY): It is one of the flagship schemes aimed at providing free-of-cost skills in 221+ job roles (offering short-term training between 2 months to 6 months)

- Pradhan Mantri Kaushal Kendra (PMKK): It is an initiative toward the creation of a "Model Training Center" with standardized infrastructure for the delivery of skill development training (719 PMKKs across all states & UTs).

- National Apprenticeship Promotion Scheme (NAPS): The scheme is aimed to increase the involvement of industries and employers in engaging youth as apprentices and providing on-the-job skill training to create a ready workforce. The government reimburses part of the stipend paid by the employer (More than 4.8 lakh candidates & 74,000 companies registered)

- National Skill Training Institute: Under this scheme, regular vocational training programs are being conducted through an Institutional Network of 18 central Institutes.

- Recognition of Prior Learning (RPL) with Best in Class Employers: RPL certifies the skills of people with prior experience or those trained informally. Since 2016, the program has benefited close to 8 lakh people across the country.

- Skill Acquisition and Knowledge Awareness for Livelihood Promotion ("SANKALP") is a program of the Ministry of Skill Development with loan assistance from the World Bank. It aims to improve short-term skill training qualitatively and quantitatively.

- Agreements and partnerships have been struck with the private sector to boost the Skill India program. **Collaborations with corporates like NASSCOM, SAP, IBM, and Adobe** helped create a curriculum aligned with the jobs of the future.

Health Services – Increase the Access, Improve the Quality, Lower the Cost

Promised

- The last healthcare policy dates back to 2002. India now needs a comprehensive healthcare policy to address the complex healthcare challenge. BJP will initiate the New Health Policy.

- Initiate the 'National Health Assurance Mission', with a clear mandate to provide universal healthcare that is not only accessible and affordable but also effective and reduces the OOP spending for the common man.

- Education and Training - We will review the role of various professional regulatory bodies in healthcare and consider setting up an overarching lean body for healthcare. High priority will be given to addressing the shortfall of healthcare professionals.

- Modernize government hospitals, upgrading infrastructure and latest technologies.

- Increase the number of medical and para-medical colleges to make India self-sufficient in human resources and set up an AIIMS-like institute in every state.

- Yoga and Ayurveda are the gifts of ancient Indian civilization to humanity, and we will increase the public investment to promote Yoga and AYUSH. We will start integrated courses for the Indian System of Medicine (ISM), modern science, and ayurgenomics. We will set up institutions and launch a vigorous program to standardize and validate Ayurvedic medicine.

- Move to a pre-emptive care model where the focus and thrust will be on child health and prevention.

- Focus on Rural Health care delivery.

- Senior Citizens' healthcare would be a special focus area.

- Give high priority to chronic diseases and will invest in research and development of solutions for chronic diseases like obesity, diabetes, cancer, CVD, etc.

- Utilize the ubiquitous platform of mobile phones for healthcare delivery and set up the 'National eHealth Authority' to leverage telemedicine and mobile healthcare to expand reach and coverage.

- Re-orientation of herbal plants board to encourage farming of herbal plants.

- Program for Women Healthcare with emphasis on rural, SC, ST, and OBC in a mission mode.

- Mission mode project to eradicate malnutrition.

- Launch National Mosquito Control mission.

- Create an open defecation-free India an awareness campaign, and enable people to build toilets in their home as well as in schools and public places.

- Set up modern, scientific sewage and waste management systems.

- We will introduce Sanitation Ratings, measuring and ranking our cities and towns on 'sanitation' and rewarding the best performers.

- Make potable drinking water available to all, thus reducing water-borne diseases, which will automatically translate into Diarrhea-free India.

Delivered

One of the most important requirements for citizens is affordable health care for all. The majority of the population still lacks access to basic healthcare systems, especially in rural areas. As per an estimate, healthcare costs land more than 5 crore India into poverty, with 3.8 crore falling below the poverty line due to spending on medicines alone. To empower "affordable health care for all," our Prime Minister Modi introduced many welfare schemes that helped poor people to get access to the health care system.

- In 2018, PM Modi launched Ayushman Bharat- one of the most ambitious health missions ever to expand universal health coverage, especially in rural and vulnerable populations.

- Four Pillars - Health and Wellness Center (HWCs), Pradhan Mantri Jan Arogya Yojana (PM-JAY), Ayushman Bharat

Digital Mission, Pradhan Mantri-Ayushman Bharat Health Infrastructure Mission.

- Rs 5 Lakhs INR of free health care cover for 50 Cr poor & vulnerable people (for Critical illness) irrespective of family size

- Allied and Healthcare Professions Bill 2018 – for regulation and standardization of education and services by allied and healthcare professionals. Setting up allied & healthcare council of India & corresponding state allied healthcare councils. Fifteen major professional categories, including 53 professions.

- Twenty new super specialty AIIMS-like hospitals are being set up. 73 Govt medical colleges upgraded. One thousand 6 hundred seventy-five hospital beds added in functional AIIMS. 15,354 MBBS seats & 12,646 PG seats increased

- 21 AIIMS have been announced to be set under the Pradhan Mantri Swasthya Suraksha Yojana (PMSSY). There is a total of 8 functional AIIMS in the country as of 2018.

- In 2014, PM Modi proposed the United Nations General Assembly to celebrate Yoga Day, which was soon accepted within a span of 3 months, and on 21 June 2015, International Yoga Day was celebrated for the first time. Two Guinness World Records were achieved- the Largest Yoga Lesson involving 35,985 participants and the maximum number of Nationalities (84) participated in a single yoga lesson.

- The National Commission for Indian System of Medicine Bill, 2019 and National Commission for Homeopathy Bill, 2019 were introduced in Rajya Sabha on 7th January 2019

- Inactivated Polio Vaccine (IPV) introduced in 2015 (6.4 Cr children benefited)

- Rotavirus Vaccine launched in March 2016 (2.6 Cr children benefited)

- The measles-rubella (MR) vaccination campaign launched in 2017 (13.04 Cr children benefited)

- Menstrual Hygiene Scheme: Implemented for adolescent girls in rural areas. Since 2014, the procurement of sanitary napkins has been decentralized. In FY 2018-19, Rs. 4254 Lakhs were allocated.

- The Rashtriya Vayoshri Yojana (RVY) scheme was Launched in 2017 to provide Physical Aids and Assisted-living Devices for Senior citizens belonging to the BPL category (70,939 senior citizens benefited)

- Modi government approved the National Health Policy 2017. The policy also seeks to "reduce premature mortality from cardiovascular diseases, cancer, diabetes or chronic respiratory diseases by 25% by 2025."

- The National Health Policy 2017 recommended the creation of the National Electronic Health Authority (NeHA) or National Digital Health Authority (NDHA) as a regulatory body for the deployment of digital health interventions in the healthcare sector (DISHA)

- MoU was signed between TRIFED (M/o Tribal Affairs) and National Medicinal Plant Board (M/o an AYUSH) to promote medicinal and aromatic plant forest produce for livelihood development among tribals.

- Govt launched the Poshan Abhiyan scheme – a first-of-its-kind initiative to tackle malnutrition through multimodal interventions. Targeted to reduce malnutrition through convergence, use of technology & a targeted approach. Rs 2122 Cr funded (2017-18,2018-19) benefiting 10 Cr people.

- Modi government has unveiled a plan to eliminate Malaria by 2030. The National Framework for Malaria Elimination (NFME) 2016-2030 document launched on 11th February 2016, lays out the vision, mission, broad principles, and practices to achieve

- Swachh Bharat Mission launched to create an open defecation-free India (More than 10 Cr toilets constructed)

- In 2016, Waste Management Rules were revised to include waste segregation into wet, dry, and hazardous waste. It also included e-waste management.

- The "Swachh Survekshan" was launched in January 2016 to measure the progress of the Swachh Bharat Abhiyan.

- The government has restructured the National Rural Drinking Water Program (NRDWP) to provide coverage to the rural population with pipe water supply and household connection ultimately by 2030

Economic Revival

Promised

- Strictly implement fiscal discipline without compromising on funds available for development work and asset creation.

- Allocate resources efficiently and effectively to re-energize the engines of growth.

- Revisit the policy framework for investments, both foreign and domestic, to make them more conducive.

- Undertake Banking reforms to enhance ease and access, as well as accountability.

- We will encourage Savings as an important driver of investment and growth.

- Delivered:

- Fiscal deficit as a percentage of GDP has been reduced from 4.5 % in 2014 to 3.4 % in the 2018-2019 year. This has been maintained without compromising on fund availability as total expenditure has increased from 18 Lakh crores in the financial year 2015-16 to 24 Lakh crores in the financial year 2018-19.

- Modi Government stood out as a performing Government; between 2014-19, the government provided a rejuvenated Center-State dynamic, cooperative federalism, GST Council, and a strident commitment to fiscal discipline. To create a new Bharat, planned and assisted by the NITI Aayog, the principle of "Reform, Perform, Transform" can succeed through many mission mode schemes implemented across the nation.

- Enhancing growth, simplicity, and transparency with GST (GST provides relief of Rs 80,000 Cr annually to consumers).

- Strong macroeconomic fundamentals define Bharat (Inflation dropped from 8.48% (in 2014) to 3.40% (in 2018)

- Banking reforms fueling the next wave of growth (Insolvency and Bankruptcy Code Insolvency helped to resolve Rs 3 lakh crore bad debts in 2 years).

- Recapitalization of PSBs by infusion of Rs 2,60,000 Cr to support credit growth & job creation.

- Sukanya Samriddhi Yojana, launched in 2015, encourages parents to start saving funds for their daughters. (More than

1.2 Cr accounts opened with more than Rs 25,979 Cr has been deposited)

- The Pradhan Mantri Jan Dhan Yojana (PMJDY) of 2014 gives citizens easy access to financial services (35 Cr people benefitted.

- Budget 2018-19 also announced certain measures to boost domestic savings, which include an increase in an exemption of interest income for senior citizens on deposits with banks and a higher limit of deduction for the health insurance premium for senior citizens.

NPAs

Promised

Will set up a strong regulatory framework for non-banking financial companies to protect the investors,

Delivered

Due to various reforms & schemes implemented by the Modi Govt, recovery made by public sector banks (PSBs) during the financial year as a percentage of gross non-performing assets (NPAs) as of the beginning of the financial year (FY) has improved from 11.33% in FY2017-18 to 13.52% in FY2018-19

Taxation

Promised

- Provide a non-adversarial and conducive tax environment.

- Rationalize and simplify the tax regime.

- Overhaul the dispute resolution mechanisms.

- Bring on board all State governments in adopting GST, addressing all their concerns.

- Provide tax incentives for investments in research and development geared toward indigenization of technology and innovation.

Delivered

- Goods and Services Tax (GST) was launched in July 2017. The GST replaced many indirect taxes with a single indirect tax. The government also made it easier to pay taxes through online portals, etc. (Rs 17 lakhs Crore collected (till Jan 2019) through GST, helping the nation implement many development initiatives).

- Modi Govt took various steps to reduce tax disputes. The monetary limits for filing appeals were increased in 2015 for a limited period. In 2015, an amendment was made to the Income Tax Act by the Finance Act to increase the limit of the Single Member Bench up to an assessed income of Rs.15 lakh. The Direct Tax Dispute Resolution Scheme came into force in 2016 and gave 7 months for settling retrospective tax disputes.

- All states & UT were brought under GST.

Foreign Direct Investment

Promised

BJP is committed to protecting the interests of small and medium retailers, SMEs, and those employed by them. The FIPBs (Foreign Investment Promotion Board) functioning shall be made more efficient and investor-friendly.

Delivered

- Prime Minister Shri Narendra Modi, in May 2017, gave his approval to the phasing out of the Foreign Investment Promotion Board (FIPB). The proposal entails abolishing the FIPB and allowing administrative Ministries/Departments to process applications for FDI requiring government approval.

- Many new initiatives like Make in India and Startup India increased FDI in Bharat. FDI jumped to 64.37 bn USD in 2017-18, with Bharat's forex reserve increasing to 422 bn USD.

Agriculture – Productive, Scientific and Rewarding

Promised

- Increase public investment in agriculture and rural development.

- Take steps to enhance the profitability in agriculture by ensuring a minimum of 50% profits over the cost of production, cheaper agriculture inputs and credit, introducing the latest technologies for farming and high-yielding seeds, and linking MGNREGA to agriculture.

- Put in place welfare measures for farmers above 60 years of age, small and marginal farmers, and farm laborers.

- Introduce and promote low water-consuming irrigation techniques and optimum utilization of water resources.

- Introduce soil assessment-based crop planning and set up mobile soil testing labs.

- Implement and incentivize the setting up of the food processing industry. We aim to set up 'agro-food processing clusters' with high value, export quality, vacuum-packed food processing facilities, etc.

- Focus on the quality, productivity, and trade of spices.

- Set up the 'Organic Farming and Fertilizer Corporation of India' to promote organic farming and fertilizers and provide incentives and support for marketing organic produce.

- Introduce rotation farming for herbal products, based on geographical mapping, to enhance farmers' incomes.

- Implement a farm insurance scheme to take care of crop loss due to unforeseen natural calamities.

- Strengthen and expand rural credit facilities.

- Promote horticulture, floriculture, pisciculture, beekeeping, and poultry to generate jobs and income for rural India.

- Promote fish farming and aquaculture. Measures would be taken for the welfare of the fisherman.

- Create Cluster-storage systems (e.g., Rice cluster, Wheat Cluster, Veg-Fruit cluster,

- Spices cluster).

- Introduce the concept of a consumer-friendly farmers' market to reduce wastage and increase incomes and risk coverage.

- Reform the APMC Act.

- Work with the states to set up seed culture labs in each district and regional agriculture innovation labs to conserve agro-biodiversity and to identify and preserve rare indigenous varieties.

- Explore the setting up of regional Kisan TV channels.

- **Give high priority to poverty alleviation in rural areas.**

Delivered

Agriculture is the primary source of livelihood for 58% of the Bharat population. As per the agriculture census, small and marginal holdings of less than 2 hectares account for 85% of total operational holdings of farming land.

Bharat has the most cultivable land in the world, followed by the United States, Russia, China, and Brazil.

It is very important to empower farmers to improve productivity and knowledge of technology & adopt new trends in agriculture to elevate the livelihood of poor farmers. Modi government's focus on "putting farmers first" empowered farmers with many initiatives, setting up a roadmap to double farmers' income by 2022. Blue Revolution & milk production increased the farmer's income. 100% urea availability significantly helped farmers to improve productivity. Modi govt. Various technology-led initiatives transformed a farmer's life.

- Record the budget allocated for farmers' welfare by the Modi Govt. (from Rs 1,21,082 Cr (2009-14) to Rs 2,11,694 Cr (2014-19).

- Many initiatives were launched to double farmers' income - like drip irrigation scheme, Soil health card, provision of quality seeds and nutrients, large investments in warehousing & cold storage chains, promotion of value addition through food processing, Online National agriculture Market, New Crop Insurance scheme.

- Schemes like Atal Pension Yojana, Ayushman Bharat, and PM Accident Insurance Scheme empowered poor farmers above the age of 60 years.

- Rs 50,000 Cr invested for Drip Irrigation Scheme (Pradhan Mantri Krishi Sinchai Yojana).

- Dedicated micro-irrigation funds of Rs 5000 Cr with over 37 lakh hectares of land covered under micro-irrigation.

- Soil Health Card scheme - Free for Farmers & covers collection of soil samples, their test, generation, and distribution of soil health cards to the farmer (18 Cr farmers benefited).

- The total output in the food processing sector increased from Rs. 9,34,272.19 crore in 2014-15 to Rs.12,76,995.11 crore in 2018-19. The number of persons engaged in the registered food processing sector increased from 17.73 lakh in 2014-15 to 20.05 lakh in 2018-19 (as per ASI).

- PM Modi inaugurated World Food India in 2017. India was showcased as the preferred investment destination in the Food Processing sector. 13 MoUs worth Rs 68,000 Cr were signed on the inaugural day.

- Pradhan Mantri Kisan Sampada Yojana (PMKSY) was launched in 2017 to supplement agriculture, modernize processing, and decrease Agri-Waste with a budget of Rs 6000 Cr.

- Paramparagat Krishi Vikas Yojana (PKVY) has been implemented in the country since 2015-16 for the country to promote chemical-free organic farming.

- 2 37,820 hectares of the area under organic farming against the target of 2 lakh hectares, and 5,94 550 farmers benefited under the scheme (Rs 582 Cr was released to states).

- The Modi Govt approved the continuation of the National AYUSH Mission (NAM) as a Centrally Sponsored Scheme from 1st April 2017 to 31st March 2020 with a financial outlay of Rs.2400.00 Crore.

- PM Mudra Loans are available for non-agricultural activities up to Rs. 10 lakh, and activities allied to agriculture, such as Dairy, Poultry, beekeeping, etc, are also covered.

- Blue Revolution Scheme (Integrated Development and Management of Fisheries was launched (2015-16) - Fishers, Fish farmers, Entrepreneurs, Cooperatives, SHGs, and other private recipients, including women, are beneficiaries.

- As of July 2018, 100 agro-processing clusters have been allocated among the states.

- Prime Minister's National agriculture Market (eNAM) is an online trading platform for agricultural commodities in Bharat. The market facilitates farmers, traders, and buyers with online trading in commodities (a total of 585 Markets).

- The government has developed and upgraded existing rural haats into Gramin Agricultural Markets (GrAMs)

- The Agricultural Produce and Livestock Marketing (Promotion and Facilitation) Act 2017 connects farmers directly to consumers.

- 130 Notified Seed Testing Laboratories, including 2 Central Seed Testing laboratories and 4 National Referral Laboratory for testing of Genetically Modified Organism and Living Modified Organisms, are working in the country.

- DD Kisan TV channel was launched in 2015.

Industry - Modern, Competitive and Caring

Promised

- We will ensure that a conducive, enabling environment is created, making 'doing business' in

- India easy.

- We will focus on cutting the red tape, simplifying the procedures, and removing the bottlenecks.

- Our attempt will be to move towards a single window system of clearances both at the center and also at the State level through a Hub-spoke model.

- We will put in place a mechanism that will ensure that the Central and state governments work in close coordination and synergy while giving clearance to mega projects.

- Decision-making on environment clearances will be made transparent as well as time bound.

- We will set up world-class Investment and Industrial regions as Global Hubs of Manufacturing.

- We will set up a task force to review and revive our MSME sector (micro and small Medium-scale enterprises), enabling it to have better access to formal credit and technology for modernization.

- Frame the environmental laws in a manner that provides no scope for confusion and will lead to speedy clearance of proposals without delay.

Manufacturing

- Increase the public spending on R&D and Incentivize R&D investments by the industry to increase the competitiveness of the manufacturing sector.

- We will facilitate the setting up of software and hardware manufacturing units.

- Encourage Indian companies to go global, and we will support Indian companies in this endeavor.

- We believe that Indian entrepreneurs have the capability to take on global markets.

- Set up trade facilitation to ensure easier customs clearances and visas for business travel.

- Initiate a government - Industry Dialogue, a channel for regular interface with the industry.

Delivered

Even though our nation has the ability, talent & potential, a big change was needed to manufacture in Bharat and make Bharat a Global Manufacturing Hub. PM Modi launched the **'Make in India'** campaign to facilitate investment, foster innovation, enhance skill development, protect intellectual property & build best in class manufacturing infrastructure.

The Prime Minister also dedicated 12 key initiatives to helping in the growth, expansion, and facilitation of MSMEs across the country:

- Bharat has made a leap from 142 rank (2014) to 77 rank (2018) in the World Bank's Ease of Doing Business Ranking 2018. Bharat ranks first in the Ease of Doing Business Report among South Asian countries compared to 6th in 2014.

- Modi Govt has streamlined regulations, removed red tape bureaucracy, and tackled corruption and tax evasion.

- Based on the World Bank's report "World Bank's Doing Business 2019", Bharat has simplified procedures in all 11 categories tracked by the World Bank.

- PM Modi has always stressed the importance of good governance with the vision of "Minimum Government and Maximum

Governance." Three hundred 72 specific business reform actions were implemented through states.

- Bharat became the world's No. 1 in Greenfield FDI Investment (2015 & 2016). Bharat climbed to 40th rank in WEF's global competitive index from 71 rank (2014-15).

- "PARIVESH" is an environmental single window hub for Environment, Forest, Wildlife, and CRZ clearances launched by PM Modi in 2018.

- Industrial corridor program - created world-class infrastructure, connectivity, and new greenfield smart cities as global manufacturing hubs, which created large employment opportunities (Delhi-Mumbai Industrial Corridor (DMIC) project).

- Based on the success of the DMIC project, the government has also started planning and development activities in 4 other industrial corridor projects, i.e., Amritsar Kolkata Industrial Corridor (AKIC), Chennai Bengaluru Industrial Corridor (CBIC), Bengaluru Mumbai Economic Corridor (BMEC) and East Coast Economic Corridor (ECEC) from Kolkata to Chennai.

- PM Modi's transformative measures, like legislative and regulatory reforms, supported startups and, lower tax rates for MSMEs, and quicker environmental clearances from 600 days to 140 days.

Manufacturing

- Modi government initiated the Impacting Research Innovation and Technology (IMPRINT) scheme in 2014 and the Uchhatar Avishkar Yojana (UAY) in 2015.

- IMPRINT focuses on research in higher educational institutions, with an allocation of Rs.487.00 crore for a period of 3 years beginning 2016-17. UAY promotes industry-sponsored, outcome-oriented research projects with an outlay of Rs.475.00 crore for a period of 2 years beginning 2016-17

- The government notified the Electronics Manufacturing Clusters (EMC) Scheme in 2017 for a period of 5 years (i.e., up to October 2022) available for disbursement of funds for the approved projects. Under the EMC scheme, 20 Greenfield EMCs and 3 Common Facility Centres (CFCs) measuring an area of 3565 acres with project cost of Rs. 3898 crore, including Government Grant-in-aid of Rs. 1577 crore have been approved in 15 states across the country.

- Mobile manufacturing units increased from 2 (2014) to 268 (2019)

- "Make In India" Launched by Prime Minister Modi on 25th September 2014 to make Bharat the hub of manufacturing, Bharat has emerged as one of the fastest-growing economies

- Bharat's share in global electronics manufacturing grew from 1.3% (2012) to 3.0% (2018)

- The Central Board of Excise & Customs launched a Single window interface for facilitating Trade (SWIFT) in April 2016 to enable exporters to file a common electronic declaration.

- The two facilitation schemes, Accredited Clients Program (ACP) and Authorized Economic Operator (AEO) have been merged into a combined three-tier AEO Program to further facilitate/ provide benefits to the exporters/ importers.

- 24X7 Customs clearance facility has been made available at 19 seaports and 17 Air Cargo Complexes. The government reduced the number of documents regarding the export/import process.

- The Digital India Scheme was launched in August 2014. It is a program to transform India into a digitally empowered society and knowledge economy.

Cooperative Sector, Handicrafts, Artisans

Promised

- Review the existing laws with regard to the cooperative sector and amend the multi-state cooperative act to remove lacunae and anomalies.

- Market linkages - both national and international

- Access to credit and information and skills upgradation

- Value addition will be encouraged through avenues like - branding, packaging, and technology.

- Schemes will be drawn for skills upgradation and enhancement of business opportunities for artisans like smiths, weavers, carpenters, hair-dressers, shoe-smiths, and potters.

Delivered

- In 2016, exercising its powers under Section 124 of the Act, Modi Govt. amended the Multi-State Cooperative Societies Rules.

- The 'Under Pehchan' initiative was launched on 7th October 2016 to register and provide Aadhar-based Identity Cards to the Handicrafts Artisans for better access to the benefits of the schemes. (17.83 Lakhs benefited).

- New Mega Clusters have been sanctioned at Bareilly, Lucknow, and Kutch with an outlay of Rs. 28.5 crores each and at J&K with an outlay of Rs. 20.00 crores.

- Special projects have been sanctioned for the Integrated Development and Promotion of Handicrafts in Jharkhand, Uttarakhand, Kerala, Madhya Pradesh, Tamil Nadu, Andhra Pradesh, Telangana, Karnataka, Bihar, Varanasi (Uttar Pradesh), benefiting 1,58,805 artisans.

- Design and Technology Upgradation: 756 programmes organized amounting to Rs. 53.33 Crores benefiting 29570 artisans.

- Marketing Support and Services: 788 programs organized amounting to Rs 87.61 Crores benefiting 58526 artisans.

- Research and Development: 702 program organized amounting to Rs 23.39 Crores benefiting 17550 artisans.

- Direct Benefit to Artisans: Rs 58.40 Crores sanctioned benefiting 478089 artisans.

- Infrastructure & Technology Support: Rs 98.76 Crores sanctioned to provide infrastructural support.

- Comprehensive Handicrafts Cluster Development (Mega Cluster): Rs. 226.65 Crores sanctioned benefiting 71915 artisans.

Services – Driven by Quality and Efficiency

Business and Trade

Promised

- Focus on Defective products.

- Build world-class ports, connecting them with roads and rail to the hinterland so as to drive the country's maritime trade.

- Air Cargo facilities will be enhanced throughout the country.

- The current accounts deficit will be brought down aggressively by focusing on exports and reducing the dependency on imports. Value addition to our products will be the biggest task.

- We shall work with the State governments to usher in the GST in an appropriate timeframe. To implement the same, a robust IT network system will be put in place.

- We will embark on the path of IPRs and Patents in a big way.

- Take all necessary steps to protect the interest of retailers, small traders, and small vendors and equip them with the latest techniques and methods to modernize them and make them competitive.

- Commit to ensuring that the retailers and SMEs don't have to spend time and money seeking multiple licenses to start the business. There will be a system in place to avoid harassment of small traders.

- Ensure easy availability of institutional credit.

- Review obsolete and multiple laws to reduce and simplify them.

- **The Telecom revolution has touched the length and breadth of the country, but there is significant scope and necessity**

to improve the quality of voice and data to fully leverage the potential.

- Delivered:

- Launched in 2016 by the Ministry of MSME, the scheme is an integrated and comprehensive certification system. As many as 23,948 Micro, Small, and Medium-sized Enterprises (MSMEs) had registered with the intent to adopt the principle of the Zero Defect Zero Effect Scheme (ZED).

- Sagarmala Project - 500 projects with an investment of more than Rs 8 lakh Crore. New 106 waterways in 4 years compared to 5 waterways in 30 years

- AAI Cargo Logistics and Allied Services Company Ltd. (AAICLAS) was incorporated on 11th August 2016 as a 100 % subsidiary of the Airports Authority of India. AAICLAS is operating 20 International and 31 Domestic Air Cargo Terminals in India and 1 Courier Facility

- The revised Foreign Trade Policy focuses on continued support for multilateral rule-based global trade. Uniform tax rates and practices across states under GST have led to huge logistics and transaction cost savings for exporters.

- Goods and Services Tax is a "One Nation One Tax" system that removes additional tax burdens on common people (customers) & brings efficient tax collection, reduction in corruption & easy inter-state movement of goods.

- The National Intellectual Property Rights (IPR) Policy 2016 was adopted with the objective "Creative India; Innovative India."

- 59-minute loan portal to enable easy access to credit for MSMEs. Mandatory 25 percent procurement from MSMEs by CPSEs

- Loans under the Pradhan Mantri Mudra Yojana (PMMY) Scheme have been extended to small/micro business enterprises since 2015, benefiting with more than Rs 6 Lakhs Crore INR financial loans distributed.

- More than 1500 obsolete laws were removed by Modi Govt.

- PM Modi approved the National Digital Communications Policy-2018. The 'Customer focused' and 'application driven' NDCP-2018 leads to new ideas and innovations after the launch of advanced technology such as 5G, IOT, M2M, etc., which shall govern the telecom sector of Bharat.

Tourism – Untapped Potential

Promised

- **To initiate a mission mode project to create 50 tourist circuits that are affordable and built around themes like a.) Archaeological and Heritage, b.) Cultural and Spiritual, c.) Himalayan, d.) Desert, e.) Coastal, f.) Medical (Ayurveda and Modern Medicine), etc. This will lead to the creation of infrastructure and employment around each tourist circuit and help boost revenue generation**.

Delivered

- PM Modi launched the Swadesh Darshan Scheme (Central Sector Scheme) with the following 5 circuits: Himalayan Circuit, North East Circuit, Krishna Circuit, Buddhist Circuit, and Coastal Circuit. Later, during 2015, 2016, and 2017, 10 more thematic circuits, namely the Desert Circuit, Tribal Circuit, Eco Circuit, Wildlife Circuit, Rural Circuit, Spiritual Circuit, Ramayana Circuit, Heritage Circuit, Tirthankar Circuit, and Sufi Circuit, were added to the scheme making it to 15 thematic circuits.

Labor Force – The Pillar of Our Growth

Promised

- Issue identity cards to the unorganized sector laborers, and arrangements will be made to provide them with good quality health and education services. Also, their skills will be upgraded through appropriate training programs.

- Extend access to modern financial services to labor - including considering the option of setting up a dedicated Workers' Bank.

- Bring together all stakeholders to review our Labor laws, which are outdated, complicated, and even contradictory.

- **Strengthen the Pension and Health Insurance safety nets for all kinds of laborers.**

Delivered

- Unorganized Workers Identification Number (UWIN) and allotment of an Aadhaar Identification number to them without issuing any smart card was approved by the Modi government with an estimated cost of Rs. 402.7 Crore, implemented in 2 years during 2017-18 and 2018-19.

- Jan Dhan Scheme (Zero balance bank accounts) empowered laborers to access modern financial services (35.75 Cr poor people benefited)

- More than 1500 obsolete laws were removed across all sectors.

- Modi Govt launched a new initiative called Atal Pension Yojana (APY) in 2015 focused on all citizens in the unorganized sector (1.5 Cr people benefited).

- PM Jan Arogya Yojana (Free Healthcare Scheme) was launched in 2018 for 50 Cr poor people with Rs 5 Lakhs annual coverage to provide comprehensive healthcare services for the poor. (28 lakhs poor people benefited)

Housing – No Longer a Mirage

Promised

- Prioritize all our resources toward this goal.

- Leverage land as a resource in urban areas and demand for unskilled labor in rural areas.

- Innovatively structure the program to converge and dovetail various existing programs while adding the missing links.

- Simultaneously, encourage the overall housing sector through appropriate policy interventions and credit availability and interest subvention schemes.

Delivered

- Pradhan Mantri Awas Yojana (Housing for All) – Urban (PMAY-U) & Rural (PMAY-G), a flagship Mission of PM Modi, was launched in 2015-2016. The Mission addressed the urban housing shortage among the EWS/LIG and MIG categories, including the slum dwellers, by ensuring a pucca house to all eligible urban households & rural houses by the year 2022 (1.5 Cr houses completed in Rural & 26 lakhs in Urban)

- To fast-track the construction of sanctioned houses, the Govt identified **24 new technologies** for mass housing construction.

- The **Affordable Housing Fund (AHF)** was established by **the National Housing Bank (NHB)** to improve the affordability of the target group to their homes.

- The huge investment of **3.6 Lakh crore** in the housing sector is providing more job opportunities in construction and allied sectors with the help of induced effect and contributing to the overall health of the economy.

- Govt. initiated the Global Housing Technology Challenge - India (GHTC-India), which aims to identify and mainstream a basket of innovative construction technologies from across the globe for the housing construction sector that is sustainable, eco-friendly, and disaster-resilient.

Physical Infrastructure – Better than the Best

Promised

- Work on the Freight Corridors and attendant Industrial Corridors will be expedited. This will result in the faster movement of people and goods.

- Remote states like those in the Northeast and Jammu and Kashmir will be connected with the rest of India through world-class highways and rail lines.

- National Highway construction projects will be expedited, especially Border and Coastal highways.

- Every village will be connected through all-weather roads.

- We shall modernize existing and operational airports and build new ones, especially connecting smaller towns and all tourism circuits. In addition, there is a potential for inland air transportation to various remote and local locations in the country. Such airstrips will be developed so that low-cost air travel becomes possible within the country.

- We will evolve an economic model of Port-led development. India is blessed with a long coastline.

- We will modernize existing ports on one hand and develop new ones on the other - stringing together our Sagar Mala project.

- Public-private partnerships would be encouraged to tap into private sector resources as well as expertise. An institutional framework would be established for the same, while regulators would be given greater autonomy as well as accountability.

Next Generation Infrastructure

- Set up Gas Grids to make gas available to households and industry.

- Set up a National Optical-Fibre Network up to the village-level and Wi-Fi zones in public areas.

- Harness our advanced satellite technology and expertise for development.

Delivered

- Modi government is developing the Delhi-Mumbai Industrial Corridor as a global manufacturing and investment destination around the 1,504 km long Western Dedicated Freight Corridor (DFC) as the backbone. Investment Regions and Industrial Areas have been identified for development in this corridor across 6 States, namely Gujarat, Haryana, Madhya Pradesh, Maharashtra, Rajasthan, and Uttar Pradesh.

- Northeast is fully integrated with the rest of Bharat & entire rail network is converted to Broad Gauge. Meghalaya, Tripura & Mizoram connected to Bharat's rail map for the first time.

- Bharat's longest road tunnel (Chenani Nashri Tunnel in Jammu) & Longest bridge, the Dhola-Sadiya bridge over the river Brahmaputra in Assam, is dedicated to the nation.

- Bharatmala Project (development of roads) with Rs 5,35,000 Cr for expanding the highways sector. National Highways' speed of construction increased from 12km per day (2013) to 27km per day (2017). National highway expanded from 92,851 km (2014) to 1,31,328 km (2017).

- Under the PM Village Roads Scheme (PM Gram Sadak Yojana), 1.56 lakh km of rural roads have been built since 2014. Rural road connectivity increased from 56% (2014) to 97% (2018).

- National Civil Aviation Policy 2016 transformed the aviation sector. PM Modi approved the proposal for the revival of 50 un-served/under-served airports/airstrips of the State governments, the Airports Authority of India (AAI), and Civil enclaves. UDAN Scheme added 40 airports.

- Under the Sagarmala Program, 415 projects, at an estimated investment of approximately Rs.8 Lac Crore, have been identified across port modernization & new port development, port connectivity enhancement, port-linked industrialization, and coastal community development for phase-wise implementation over the period 2015 to 2035.

- The implementation plan of the Sagarmala Program, to be taken up through private/PPP mode.

Next Generation Infrastructure

- **National Gas Grid (Pradhan Mantri Urja Ganga):** To have a gas-based economy and enhance the share of gas in the energy basket to 15%, the Modi government has envisaged developing an additional 15,000 km of gas pipeline network (8 Cr poor women received free LPG connection under PM Ujjwala Scheme).

- The natural gas grid in the country connects the western, northern, and southeastern gas markets with primary gas sources. As a commitment to provide clean energy in the Eastern part of the country, the government has approved a capital grant of Rs. 5,176 Crore.

- 1,19,122 Gram Panchayats connected by optical fiber. Under National Digital Communications Policy 2018, Wi-Fi Hotspots at each Gram Panchayat facilitate the utilization of the infrastructure established by BharatNet.

- To promote the use of space technology for governance and public administration, the Department of Space formed expert working groups in ISRO for proactive interaction with the government departments and prepared the joint action plan on "Effective use of Space Technology in Governance & Development."

Transport

Promised

- Create a public transport system that can reduce the dependence on personal vehicles for transport, thereby reducing cost, time to travel, and ecological cost.

- Launch an Integrated Public transport project, including roadways, railways, and waterways.

- Develop waterways for passenger and cargo transport.

- Develop a National logistics network for faster movement of goods.

- Delivered

- **The metro network has risen to 18 cities from 5 in 2014. With a focus on reducing carbon footprint while enhancing road safety, efficiency, and convenience for road users, An MoU was signed with 'Transport for London (TFL) to revamp the public transport system in the country.**

- **Bharatmala & Sagarmala Projects launched for overall roadways & Waterways connectivity.**

- **One hundred 6 new waterways have been added since 2014 (only 5 National waterways in the last 30 years).**

- On the three-day India Integrated Transport and Logistics Summit conducted by Govt, Thirty-four MoUs amounting to about Rs 2 lakh crores were signed.

Railways

Promised

- Hinterland will be connected to the ports through strategic new Rail networks.

- Agri Rail network will be established - with Train Wagons designed to cater to the specific needs of perishable Agricultural products like milk and vegetables as well as lightweight wagons for salt movement.

- Tourist Rail - including Pilgrimage Rail.

- Railways Modernization, inducting of state-of-the-art technology.

- Prioritize Safety and invest in the required overhaul of stressed infrastructure, strict norms, and warning systems.

- Modernize and equip all stations with requisite infrastructure and public utilities.

- Convert all unmanned crossings into manned crossings in a phased manner.

- Initiate R&D for indigenous railways, coach design, and signals.

- We will launch the Diamond Quadrilateral project - of the High-Speed Train network (bullet train)

Delivered

- The Sagarmala Program saw the completion of 89 projects, while 443 projects worth Rs. 4.32 lakh crore are under various stages of implementation and development. Indian Port Rail Corporation Limited (IPRCL) has taken up 32 works (cost: Rs. 18,253 cr) across 9 major ports, of which 8 works (Rs. 175 cr) have been completed. In addition, 23 rail connectivity projects (Rs. 24,877 Cr) identified under Sagarmala are being taken up by the Ministry of Railways.

- Parcel Cargo Express Train (PCET) began operation in 2018, connecting the Northeast to the West Coast. Parcel Cargo Express Train enables farmers to market their products like tea, betel nuts, pineapple, jute, horticulture products, cane furniture, etc., at the retail markets in Mumbai, Bengaluru, Nagpur, Pune.

- **Vistadome Coaches & Hill Railways:** These coaches are provided with an enhanced viewing area, including on the roof, to enable tourists to enjoy a panoramic view while traveling. In December 2018, Railways notified the Indian Railways Heritage Charter (IRHC) -2018 for the first time in its history.

- Modern **Deen Dayalu Coaches** manufacturing (more than 1100 Deen Dayalu coaches have been manufactured). Ultra-modern Tejas Trains with speed potential up to 200 km.

- **Enhanced Safety**: Induction of technology for safety improvements – Smart Coach, online Monitoring of Rolling Stock (OMRS), Complete switchover to LHB, Elimination of Level Crossings, New Initiatives In Track Maintenance.

- More than 65 stations across Zonal railways have been beautified under the Station Beautification initiative by using local art forms, painting styles, and local themes. Brighter and energy-efficient railways with 100% LED lights at all Railway Stations.

- All 8948 unmanned level crossings at broad gauge routes have been eliminated (2 years ahead of target).

- R&D: Streamlining of the vendor registration process of RDSO, Collaboration with Other Research and Academic Institutions (IITs).

- First ever bullet train project in Bharat: Mumbai – Ahmedabad high-speed rail.

Water – Make It Reach to All Homes, Farms and Factories

Promised

- Launch the 'Pradhan Mantri Gram Sinchayee Yojana' with the motto 'har khet ko paani.' We will launch a multi-pronged' water strategy' for reducing farmers' dependence on monsoons. Increase irrigated land by completing the long pending irrigation projects on priority.

- We will nurture groundwater recharge by harnessing rainwater to reduce dependence on groundwater.

- Encourage efficient use, water conservation, recycling, and rainwater harvesting.

- Sewage treatment plants to prevent the pollution of rivers.

- Desalination plants for drinking water supply in coastal cities

- Interlinking of rivers based on feasibility.

- Examination of groundwater to eliminate toxic chemicals, particularly arsenic and fluorides.

- Encourage setting up of drinking water supply grid in water-scarce areas.

- Promote decentralized, demand-driven, community-managed water resource management, water supply, and environmental sanitation.

- Facilitate piped water to all households.

Delivered

- Drip Irrigation Scheme (PMKSY) – Rs 50,000 Cr investment, over 37 lakh hectares under micro-irrigation (2015-16).

- Central Ground Water Board (CGWB), in the year 2018, took up Artificial Recharge work in 3 aspirational districts: Osmanabad, Maharashtra, YSR Kadapa district, Andhra Pradesh, and Jangaon district, Telangana.

- Surface Minor Irrigation (SMI) and Repair, Renovation, and Restoration (RRR) of Water Bodies scheme (Rs 101 Cr released to states 2017 & 2018)

- Under the Namami Gange program, a total of 254 projects worth Rs.24,672 crore have been sanctioned for various activities, including sewage infrastructure. One hundred 31 projects were sanctioned for the creation of 3076 MLD new sewage treatment plants (STPs) and the rehabilitation of 887 MLD of existing STPs.

- The seawater desalination plant was under construction in Odisha's coastal district of Ganjam. Another in Kalpakkam, Chennai, is already in operation.

- A National Perspective Plan for Water Resources Development was launched in December 2015 to conduct a feasibility study on interlinking rivers. By March 2018, 30 links had been identified as feasible.

- The government conducts the Minor Irrigation (MI) census in order to create a sound and reliable database on groundwater and surface water Minor Irrigation Schemes in the country.

- As per the World Water Council (WWC) in 2017, the drinking water standards have improved in the last 5 years.

- National Aquifer Management (NAQUIM): mapping of water-bearing aquifers has been planned with an aim to enhance the capacity of states in Ground Water Management and Development

- The government restructured the National Rural Drinking Water Program (NRDWP) to reach the goal of increasing coverage of sustainable Piped Water Supply.

Energy – Generate More, Use Rationally, Waste Less

Promised

- Come out with a responsible and comprehensive 'National Energy Policy.'

- Focus on the development of energy infrastructure, human resource development, and upgradation of technology.

- Take steps to maximize the potential of oil, gas, hydel power, ocean, wind, coal, and nuclear.

- Sources. BJP considers energy efficiency and conservation crucial to energy security.

- Set up small hydro power generation projects to harness the hydropower that is not being used at the moment. Small projects can be set up with local support and without displacement of the local population.

- Take Steps to increase domestic coal exploration and production to bridge the demand and supply gap. Oil and gas explorations would also be expedited in the country. This will also help to reduce the import bill.

- Give a thrust to renewable sources of energy as an important component of India's energy mix.

- Expand and strengthen the national solar mission.

Delivered

- The 4 key objectives of the New Energy Policy are access at affordable prices, improved energy security and independence, greater sustainability, and economic growth. The policy is being discussed by NITI Aayog with different stakeholders (2016)

- In 2017, the Saubhagya Scheme was announced to provide electricity to every household in Bharat (2.62 Cr households electrified). This includes setting up energy infrastructure.

- The National Offshore Wind Energy Policy was notified in 2015, and the NITI Aayog put out a draft of a National Energy Policy in 2017. The government amended the Atomic Energy Act in 2015

- A total of around 73.35 GW of renewable energy capacity has been installed in the country as of October 2018 from all renewable energy sources, which includes around 34.98 GW from Wind, 24.33 GW from solar, 4.5 GW from Small Hydro Power and 9.54 GW from Bio-power.

- 105 MT increase in coal production in 4 years (2014-18). 89 Coal Mines have been transparently auctioned and allotted with 100% revenues to coal-bearing states,

- International Solar Alliance (ISA) was launched jointly by PM Modi and the President of France on 30th November 2015, with 121 countries as members.

- The government approved the National Wind-Solar Hybrid Policy on 14th May 2018 to provide a framework for the promotion of large grid-connected wind-solar PV hybrid systems for optimal and efficient utilization of wind and solar resources, transmission infrastructure, and land.

Science and Technology – India Innovates and India Leads

Promised

- Mounting a direct and sustained effort on the alleviation of poverty by using scientific and technological capabilities along with our traditional knowledge pool.

- Encouraging research and innovation in areas of relevance for the economy and society

- Promoting international science and technology cooperation toward achieving the goals of national development and security and making it a key element of our international relations.

- Devise schemes, programs, and opportunities to encourage the youth to take scientific research and innovation as a career.

- Provide work environment and professional opportunities in fundamental scientific research.

- Build world-class, regional centers of excellence of scientific research in the fields of nanotechnology, material sciences, thorium technology, and brain research.

- Create an ecosystem for multi-country and inter-disciplinary collaborative research, and establish an Intellectual Property Rights Regime.

- Achieving synergy between industry and scientific research.

- Promotion of innovation by creating a comprehensive national system of innovation.

- Indigenous knowledge, based on our long and rich tradition, will be further developed and harnessed for the purpose of wealth and employment generation.

- To promote science popularization schemes extensively.

- Bring the changes in secondary education to focus on the application of science.

- Set up an institute of big data and Analytics to study the impact of big data across sectors for predictive science.

- To do research for the eradication of tropical diseases.

- Establish institutes of Technology for Rural Development.

- Establish a Central University dedicated to Himalayan Technology.

- Promote research and application of nuclear science in medicines, industry, and agriculture.

Delivered

- Modi Govt launched a program called Unnat Bharat Abhiyan with an aim to connect institutions of higher education, including Indian Institutes of Technology (IITs), National Institutes of Technology (NITs), and Indian Institutes of Science Education & Research (IISERs)

- The government instituted several schemes/programs aimed at encouraging young scientists to engage themselves in scientific activities / undertake research work. (Example - Innovation in Science Pursuit for Inspired Research (INSPIRE))

- Govt. approved the launch of the National Mission on Interdisciplinary Cyber-Physical Systems (NM-ICPS) implementation at a total outlay of Rs. 3660 crore for a period of 5 years

- Teacher Associateship for Research Excellence (TARE), Overseas Visiting Doctoral Fellowship (OVDF).

- 1st ASEAN-India InnoTech Summit was hosted by Bharat in 2018.

- National Initiative for Developing and Harnessing Innovations (NIDHI) 2016 - NIDHI comprises various components that provide a comprehensive framework for promoting and accelerating innovation-driven enterprises across the nation.

- The National Intellectual Property Rights (IPR) Policy 2016 was adopted in May 2016 as a vision document to guide future development of IPRs in the country.

- Bharat – UK Science & Innovation Policy 2018 to scale up collaboration to tackle global challenges, realizing the potential of artificial intelligence (AI), digital economy, health technologies, and cyber security.

- A Draft Policy Document, Scientific Research Infrastructure and Maintenance Networks (SRIMAN) in the S&T sector has already been framed by Govt.

- Bharat is working & committed to eliminating Neglected Tropical Diseases (NTDs) like Lymphatic Filariasis (Hathipaon) and Visceral Leishmaniases (Kala-Azar)

- School of Agro and Rural Technology at IIT Guwahati was established in the year 2016.

- The Department of Atomic Energy has been conducting research and development activities in the field of food and agriculture. The 2018-19 budget increased to Rs 16595 Cr compared to Rs 7700 Cr (2014)

Flora, Fauna and Environment – Safeguarding Our Tomorrow

Promised

- Cleaner fuels will be promoted so as to bring down pollution levels, particularly in the cities.

- The concept of proactive 'Carbon Credit' will be promoted.

- Ecological Audit of projects and pollution indexing of cities and townships will be done on

- scientific basis.

- In addition to protecting the existing forests and wildlife reserves, the wastelands of the country will be used for social forestry.

- Guidelines for Green buildings and energy-efficient workplaces will be brought out.

- R&D and Human Resource Development in Environment Technology will be promoted.

- Set up foolproof mechanisms for the protection and preservation of wildlife.

- Encourage citizens' participation in reforestation, agroforestry, and social forestry through targeted programs.

- Encourage and incentivize innovative garbage disposal and waste management practices, especially recycling techniques.

- The Himalayas

- Launch 'National Mission on Himalayas' as a unique program of inter-governmental Partnership in coordinated policy-making and capacity-building across states and sectors.

- Create a 'Himalayan Sustainability Fund'.

- Give due Importance to the programs devised to arrest the melting of Himalayan glaciers from which most of the rivers in North India originate.

Delivered

- PM Modi approved the National Policy on Biofuels – 2018. The Policy categorizes biofuels as "Basic Biofuels." Under this program, an indicative target of 20% blending of ethanol in petrol by 2025 was laid out.

- Faster Adoption and Manufacturing of (Hybrid &) Electric Vehicles in Bharat (FAME India) Scheme in 2015 to promote the adoption of electric/ hybrid vehicles (EVs) in Bharat with a budget of Rs 895 Cr.

- Govt. Launched a New Website on the National Clean Development Mechanism Authority (http://www.ncdmaindia.gov.in). Delhi metro, which has become India's first MRTS project to earn carbon credits, has the potential to reduce about 0.57 million tonnes of CO_2 e annually.

- During the year 2018, many important bilateral and multilateral meetings and negotiations on climate change were held in the run-up to the 24th Conference of the Parties to UNFCCC (COP-24)

- Under the National Adaptation Fund on Climate Change **(NAFCC),** 27 projects (including one regional project) have been approved at a total cost of Rs. 673.63 crore.

- Projects under the Watershed Development Component of Pradhan Mantri Krishi Sinchayee Yojana (WDC-PMKSY), principally for the development of rainfed portions of the cultivated area and wastelands, are evaluated for implementation.

- Govt released Model Building Bye-Laws in 2016, which advocates various norms for green buildings. The Bureau of Energy Efficiency (BEE) published guidelines for the design and construction of energy-efficient buildings in 2017.

- **Four Projects selected in real-time air and water quality monitoring (2018) -** These research projects will be pursued by leading Indian scientific and technical institutions such as IITs and IISc in collaboration with top US institutions like Duke University, University of South California, Michigan State University, Stanford University, etc.

- **Wildlife protection -** Total outlay is Rs. 1731.72 crores as central share (Rs. 1143 crore for Project Tiger, Rs. 496.50 crores for Development of Wildlife Habitats, and Rs.92.22 crore for Project Elephant) from 2017-18 to 2019-20.

- Green Good Deeds is the societal movement launched by Govt to protect the environment and promote good living in the country through the participation of citizens.

- **Green Skill Development Program (GSDP): More than** 30 skilling programs were conducted in 2018.

- Modi Govt. launched the Atal Mission for Rejuvenation and Urban Transformation (AMRUT) in 500 cities on June 25, 2015, with the objective of improving sewerage coverage and septage management and providing safe drinking water universally in all Urban Local Bodies (ULBs) with a population of one lakh or more.

The Himalayas

- The National Mission on Himalayan Studies (NMHS) was launched by the Ministry of Environment, Forest, and Climate Change in 2015

- More than Rs 85 Cr grant was given for various Himalayan development & preservative large & medium projects (https://nmhs.org).

- The government has carried out studies and maintains data regarding the melting of glaciers in the Indian Himalayan region. A state-of-the-art field research station, 'Himansh,' was established in the Chandra basin and has been operational since 2016 for conducting field experiments and expeditions to glaciers.

Natural & National Resources – Use When Required, Protect Where Necessary

Promised

- We will set in place national policies on critical natural resources.

- State governments will be taken into confidence in harnessing these resources.

- We will implement an auction of precious resources through efficient mechanisms, including e-auction.

- Resource mapping, exploration, and management will be undertaken through the use of technology.

- **Value addition will be encouraged in all resources instead of just marketing.**

Delivered

- In 2015, the government passed the Coal Mines (Special Provisions) Bill to provide for the allocation of coal mines.

- In 2017, the Coal Blocks Allocation Rules were added to the Mines and Minerals (Development and Regulation) Act. The Ministry of Mines amended the Mineral Auction Rules 2015 in November 2017.

- 89 Coal Mines have been transparently auctioned and allotted with 100% revenues to coal-bearing states.

- Geological Survey of India (GSI) took up 194 mineral exploration programs in different parts of the country. Resources at-2A, a powerful imaging system for resource survey, was successfully launched into space by ISRO in 2016.

- Six CEOs Pledge Support to Reduce Single-use Plastic at The Plenary Session of World Environment Day 2018.

Secure Indians – Zero Tolerance on Terrorism, Extremism and Crime

Promised

Internal Security

- Revive the anti-terror mechanism that has been dismantled by Congress, strengthen the role of NIA, and put a system in place for a swift and fair trial of terror-related cases.

- Reform the National Security Council to make it the hub of all sector-related assessments. It will be accountable for real-time intelligence dissemination. Digital and Cyber security will be a thrust area.

- Completely revamp the intelligence gathering system by modernizing the intelligence department.

- Provide the State governments with all assistance to modernize their respective police forces and equip them with the latest technology. This will be taken up on a mission mode approach.

- Strengthen and expand the Civil Defense and Home Guards mechanism to create a group of citizens for community defense, self-defense, and disaster management.

- Encourage and strengthen NCC training at the college and University levels.

- Chalk a national plan in consultation and participation of the state governments to address the challenges posed by the Maoist insurgency. Talks with the insurgent groups will be conditional and within the framework of the constitution.

- Take urgent steps for the safety of the migrant workers and communities from the Northeast and other states.

Delivered

- Bharat has taken steps to set up Joint Working Groups (JWGs) on counter terrorism/security matters with other countries. Bilateral treaties on Mutual Legal Assistance (MLATs) have also been signed with other countries. In 2017, the Counter Terrorism and Counter Radicalization Division and the Cyber and Information Security Division were created in the Ministry of Home Affairs. Nine special NIA courts have been notified since 2014.

- In 2015, The National Cyber Coordination Centre (NCCC) was approved by the government to coordinate intelligence gathering between agencies and handle issues related to national security. The government has been holding training sessions on cyber forensics through various departments and schemes like The Information Security Education and Awareness portal, cert-in, The Training Division of the Bureau of Police Research & Development, the Cyber Crime Prevention Against Women and Children scheme, CBI, etc.

- The National Cyber Coordination Centre (NCCC) was approved by Govt in 2015 to coordinate intelligence gathering between agencies and handle issues related to national security. Phase I of NCCC has been made operational since 2017.

- More than 18000 Cr were sanctioned to modernize police forces across the nation. The Crime and Criminal Network and Systems (CCTNS) has been rolled out nationally as of November 2018.

- Govt. launched the 'Plan Scheme of Mainstreaming Civil Defense in Disaster Risk Reduction' in 2014 with Rs 290 crore for Civil Defense. The number of rural districts covered under this scheme will increase from 100 to 240 districts.

- Govt. periodically updates the NCC training directives. As per the Annual Report 2018-19, against the total enrolled strength of 13,29,202 cadets, Girl Cadets were 4,23,464, constituting 31.8 % of the total enrolled cadets.

- Left Wing Extremism (LWE) incidents were reduced by 60%. Naxalism & Left Wing violence were removed from 44 districts. Maximum youths influenced by Naxal-Maoist ideology surrendered & joined the mainstream.

- Bezbaruah Committee – formed by Govt in 2014 to address concerns of the persons hailing from the Northeastern states who are living in different parts of the country. The committee recommendations have been accepted and are at various stages of implementation.

External Security – Its Boundary, Beauty and Bounty

Promised

- Address the issue of reforms with regard to defense equipment, support services, organizational reforms, and other related matters.

- Address the increasing shortage of commissioned and non-commissioned staff in the defense forces on a priority basis in a time-bound manner.

- Implement one rank, one pension.

- Build a War Memorial to recognize and honor the gallantry of our soldiers.

- Take measures to make the Short Service Commission more attractive.

- Set up the National Maritime Authority, which will be equipped with the best infrastructure and will focus on coastal security.

- Modernize armed forces and increase the R&D in defense, with a goal of developing indigenous defense technologies and fast-tracking defense purchases.

- Deal with cross-border terrorism with a firm hand.

- Review and improve the border management. Punitive measures will be introduced to check illegal immigration.

- Set up 4 dedicated defense universities to meet the shortage of manpower.

- Appoint a Veterans Commission to address the grievances of veterans, including reforming ECHS and re-employment of ex-servicemen.

- Ensure greater participation of the Armed Forces in the Ministry of Defense's decision-making process.

- Implement measures to improve the efficiency of Armed Forces Tribunals and minimize appeals by the government.

- Ensure that servicemen can register and vote from their place of posting.

- **Initiate the process of digitization of defense land in cantonment and in other places**.

Delivered

- In 2016, the Defense Procurement Procedures were amended, focusing on simplifying procedures to boost the government's 'Make in India' Initiative through indigenous design, development, and manufacturing of defense equipment, platforms, and systems.

- Modi Govt took many initiatives to include sustained image projection, participation in career fairs and exhibitions, and publicity campaigns to create awareness among the youth. Various steps are also being taken to make the armed forces jobs attractive.

- In 2018, Modi Govt implemented One Rank One Pension (OROP) for Defense Forces Personnel with effect from 01.07.2014. As on 30.09.2017 (compiled till 01.05.2018), a sum of Rs.10,795.40 crores has been released to 20,60,220 Defense Forces Pensioners / Family Pensioners

- On 25th February 2019, PM Modi inaugurated the National War Memorial at India Gate

- The IAF has recently revised the Short Service Commission (SSC) scheme to induct women into the fighter stream on an experimental basis for a period of 5 years. The first batch of 3 women officers were commissioned into the fighter stream in 2016.

- In addition to undertaking maritime surveillance in the Maritime Zone of Bharat, ICG ships and aircraft are also deployed to undertake maritime surveillance of coastal states. Sagarmala Scheme delivered many coastal maritime developmental projects.

- Govt introduced many amendments to the Defense Procurement Procedure (DPP) to ensure the increase of Indigenous manufacturing capacity (building War ships, defense aircraft, and allied items of defense equipment). Three military agencies were created - Defense Cyber Agency, Defense Space Agency & Special Operation Division Under the command of the Chairman – Chief of the Staff committee. The $5 bn S400 missile deal was signed with Russia by Modi Govt.

- Govt follows "Zero Tolerance Policy" towards cross-border terrorism.

- Implementation of Comprehensive Integrated Border Management Systems (CIBMS)to protect our nation's borders with the latest technology.

- Govt is working on converting Bharat's Central University to National Defense University.

- To appoint a Veterans Commission, the National Commission for Ex-Servicemen Bill 2015 has been drafted in order to set up the National Commission for Ex-Servicemen.

- Orders were issued for the empanelment of 85 medical facilities with ECHS in January 2018.

- The Govt enhanced the financial decision-making powers of the Vice Chiefs of the 3 defense services in order to expedite the decision-making process involved in the revenue procurements of the forces.

- In 2018, the Army launched the newest bench of the Armed Forces Tribunal (AFT) in Jammu.

- In 2016, the government amended the Conduct of Elections Rules, 1961, to enable service voters to cast their vote in elections through an e-postal ballot.

- Computerization of land records contained in the General Lands Register (GLR) and Military Lands Register (MLR), maintained by Defense Estate Officers (DEO) and Cantonment Boards, has already been completed. The Director General of Defense Estates is implementing a project for indexing, scanning, and digitization of land records contained in files of DEOs and Cantonment Boards.

Defense Production

Promised

- Technology transfer in defense manufacturing will be encouraged to the maximum.

- We will find solutions to the problems hampering the growth of the defense sector.

- We will encourage the domestic industry to have a larger share in the design and production of military hardware and platforms for both domestic use and exports in a competitive environment.

Delivered

- Govt. launched 'Mission Raksha Gyan Shakti' on November 27, 2018. The main idea behind this is to migrate from the culture of seeking Transfer of Technology (ToT) from foreign sources to generating Intellectual Property in Bharat to achieve the goal of self-reliance in the Defense sector.

- The government signed 128 defense contracts worth Rs 1.1 Lakhs Crore with various domestic industries to promote manufacturing in India.

Independent Strategic Nuclear Program

Promised

- Study in detail India's nuclear doctrine and revise and update it to make it relevant to the challenges of current times.

- Maintain a credible minimum deterrent that is in tune with changing geostatic realities.

- **Invest in India's indigenous Thorium Technology Program.**

Delivered

- In 2015, Govt amended the Atomic Energy Act of 1962, which enabled the Nuclear Power Corporation of India (NPCIL) to form joint venture companies with Indian PSUs and government sector companies.

- Govt follows a two-pronged independent nuclear program, unencumbered by foreign pressure and influence, for civilian and military purposes, especially as nuclear power is a major contributor to Bharat's energy sector.

- In December 2016, Govt accorded in-principle approval for the Tarapur Maharashtra Site (TMS) for locating a 300 MW Advanced Heavy Water Reactor that is used for thorium application. Rs.292 Crore has been allotted for the research and development program on thorium-based reactors.

Foreign Relations – Nation First, Universal Brotherhood

Promised

- Equations will be mended through pragmatism and a doctrine of mutually beneficial and interlocking relationships based on enlightened national interest.

- We will champion uniform international opinion on issues like Terrorism and Global Warming.

- Instead of being led by big power interests, we will engage proactively on our own with countries in the neighborhood and beyond.

- We will work toward strengthening Regional forums like SAARC and ASEAN.

- We will continue our dialogue, engagement, and cooperation with global forums like BRICS and G20.IBSA, SCO, and ASEM.

- We will expand and empower our pool of diplomats, ensuring our message is taken to the world, and our great nation is represented on the whole in a befitting manner.

- The NRIs, PIOs, and professionals settled abroad are a vast reservoir to articulate national interests and affairs globally.

- India shall remain a natural home for persecuted Hindus, and they shall be welcome to seek refuge here.

Delivered

- PM Modi has struck the fine balance of continuing relations as well as cultivating fresh ties, proving strategically significant in the medium and long-term, characterized by proactive, ambitious, and innovative diplomacy with the underlying theme of 'Bharat First.'

- Bharat continued to hold structured consultations through Joint Working Groups on Counter Terrorism (JWG-CT) with 23 various partner countries. Bharat played a leading role in COP21 Paris 2015.

- Bharat's agile diplomacy is marked by the policies of 'Acting east' and 'Looking west.'

- Bharat has been steadfast in its commitment to sharing the fruits of technological advances & National Knowledge Network with like-minded SAARC countries in its neighborhood (South Asia Satellite, South Asian University, Disaster Management)

- PM Modi consistently led Bharat's strong foreign policy on Economic & Finance Cooperation, Global Economic governance, and International Peace and Security with BRICS and G20.IBSA, SCO, and ASEM.

- The Economic Diplomacy Division focuses on the economic aspects of the country's foreign policy. It undertook a number of initiatives during the financial year 2018-19. Efforts were made to ensure greater coordination between the MEA, central government ministries/departments, state governments, business chambers, and missions/posts abroad.

- Govt's initiatives toward the diaspora are two-pronged. For one, they cater to the needs of NRIs and OCIs by providing them with consular services and protection and conducting outreach activities to engage with them. Second, they create policies to encourage the diaspora to contribute to India's growth through philanthropy, knowledge transfers, investments in innovation, and assistance in other development projects.

- A new citizenship amendment bill introduced in the Indian parliament in July 2016 proposes easing the path to citizenship for Hindus fleeing persecution in Afghanistan, Pakistan, and Bangladesh.

Cultural Heritage

Ram Mandir

Promised

BJP reiterates its stand to explore all possibilities within the framework of the constitution to facilitate the construction of the Ram Temple in Ayodhya.

Delivered

- Modi Govt. strongly believed in our constitution & continued to follow the legal framework for Ram Temple construction.

Ram Setu

Promised

Ram Setu is a part of our cultural heritage and is also of strategic importance due to its vast thorium deposits. These facts will be taken into consideration while making any decision on the 'Sethu_Samudram Channel' project.

Delivered

- Modi Govt. files affidavit in Supreme Court saying it will not damage the Ram Setu, intends to explore an alternative to the earlier alignment of Sethusamudram Ship Channel project.

Ganga

Promised

The River Ganga is a symbol of faith in India. A massive 'Clean Rivers Program' will be launched across the country driven by people's participation.

Delivered

- Two hundred 54 projects worth Rs 25,500 Cr sanctioned under the Namami Ganga Program. 131 projects sanctioned for 3076 MLD new sewage treatment plants (STPs)

Cow and its Progeny

Promised

- A necessary legal framework will be created to protect and promote cows and their progeny.

- A National Cattle Development board will be set up to implement a Program for the improvement of indigenous livestock breeds.

Delivered

- In 2014, the Rashtriya Gokul Mission was launched for the development and conservation of indigenous breeds, genetic upgradation of the bovine population, and enhancement of milk production.

Heritage Sites

Promised

- We will provide appropriate resources for the maintenance and restoration of all national heritage sites and to prevent their vandalization in any form.

- The digitization of archives and archaeological and museological records would be initiated.

- A National Mission for beautifying and improving the infrastructure and amenities at pilgrimage centers of all faiths will be launched.

Delivered

- The PRASAD scheme provides Central Financial Assistance for infrastructure development and beautification of tourist spots. A total of 24 projects in 15 states have been approved, with an estimated expenditure of Rs. 727.16 crore

- A 3D digitization Pilot project has been initiated to take it to another level. This project, once completed, will be a pioneering effort in the field of museum experience.

- Bharat has managed to get inscribed 7 of its properties/sites on the World Heritage List of UNESCO & has overall 37 World Heritage Inscriptions with 29 Cultural, 07 Natural, and 01 Mixed sites. Bharat India stands second largest after China in terms of the number of World Heritage properties in the ASPAC (Asia and Pacific) region; it is sixth in the world overall.

Languages

Promised

Promote Indian languages and put measures in place for the development of all Indian languages so that they become a powerful vehicle for creating a knowledge society.

Delivered

- PM Modi promoted many of our Bharat languages across the global forum & enabled many MoUs with developed countries showcasing the value of our regional languages.

Uniform Civil Code

Promised

We reiterate our stand to draft a Uniform Civil Code, drawing upon the best traditions and harmonizing them with the modern times.

Delivered

- In July 2016, Govt had asked a Law Commission panel to examine the possibility of a Uniform Civil Code.

Summary
(Modi Government – Term 1
(2014 – 2019) – Delivered Change)

Let us rewind our memory back to the year 2013;

- Bharat was called the "Capital of Corruption."

- 7 Cr poor women suffered without LPG Gas.

- 10 Cr poor people did not have access to toilets.

- 35 Cr poor people could not have access to banks.

- 19 Cr poor people could not afford insurance (life & accident).

- 20 Cr poor farmers did not know their farmland soil health.

- 14 Cr poor farmers could not get crop insurance.

- Rs 90,000 Cr INR of government subsidy money for poor people looted.

- 18,600+ villages did not have electricity

- 1,76,000 Km of village roads not constructed

- 24 Lakhs ex-servicemen & 6 lakhs war widows could not get One Rank One Pension (OROP)

- 2.5 Cr pensioners needed to walk to office to get pension money

- 18 Cr people could not afford to start small businesses despite having talents

- 1.2 Cr Pregnant women could not get proper health care

- 3 lakh fake companies operated

So, if we measure the nation's development growth pace with the speed of 2013, Bharat would have taken another 60 YEARS to complete the above targets.

Since the nation was blessed with an honest Prime Minister, Shri Narendra Modi, in May 2014, Bharat has progressed rapidly. Five years of GOOD GOVERNANCE by PM Modi at a record performance speed achieved the above-mentioned challenges in just 60 MONTHS.

"We are pledged to the services not for any community or section but for the entire nation. Every countryman is the blood of our blood and flesh of our flesh. We shall not rest till we are able to give to every one of them a sense of pride that they are children of Bharat Mata."

- Pandit Deendayal Upadhyaya

Every word of Pandit Deendayal Upadhyaya became a reality under the leadership of our Hon'ble Prime Minister Modi.

Good governance is the hallmark of any democracy. From day one, the Modi government has made good governance a top priority.

Take any central government scheme, for instance; the focus is on empowering those who are at the last mile. It is the Modi government's endeavor to strengthen the hands of the poor and bring them to the mainstream of development.

Prime Minister Modi's Term 1 (2014-2019) Good Governance delivered historic & holistic development for the first time across empowering the poor, Farmers First, Women Empowerment, Youth-focused, strong foreign relations, eliminating Corruption, transforming the Health sector, etc.

The following segment showcases the historic transformational CHANGE - DELIVERED by PM Modi.

Speed and Scale of Transformation

Unprecedented Speed Scale & Safety in Rail Development

- Train accidents reduced from 118 (2013) to 46 (2018)

- 50% increase in railway track renewals

- Broad Gauge lines commissioned 9528 Km (2014 -2018) compared to 7600 (2009-14)

- 100% electrification of broad gauge routes of Bharat Railways (fuel bill savings of Rs 13,510 Cr per annum)

Connecting Bharat at Express Pace

- Rural road connectivity increased from 56% (2014) to 97% (2018) across villages

- The speed of highway construction increased from 12 km/day (2013) to 27 km/day (2017)

- No of toilets built in rural households increased from 6.5 Cr (1947-2014) to 9.91 Cr (2014-2018)

- Gram Panchayats connected by Optical Fiber – From 59 (2011-2014) to 1.21 Lakhs (2014-2018)

- 1.8 Cr houses constructed across rural & urban areas

Unprecedented Scale of Transformation in Telecom Sector

- Broadband connections increased from 61 Million (2014) to 412 Million (2018)

- Internet coverage increased from 251 million (2014) to 446 million (2018)

- 5 Fold jump in FDI in just 3 years (USD $1.3 bn in 2015 to USD $6.2 bn in 2017)

Infrastructure for New Bharat

Next Generation Infra for New Bharat

- Bharatmala Scheme Phase I – 5.35 Lakhs crore for expanding the highways sector with multi-modal integration

- Setu Bhartam project for safer roads – making all National highways free from railway-level crossings

- Bharats's longest road tunnel (Jammu) & longest bridge (Assam)

Thrust to Environment Friendly & Cheaper Fuel

- Foundation Stone laid for City Gas Distribution (CGD) projects in 129 districts.

- 2 Crore PNG connections & 4600 CNG stations to be installed to cover 70% population.

- CGD Projects in 96 cities benefited 46.5 lakh households & 32 lakh CNG vehicles.

Harnessing Inland Waterways

- National waterways increased from 5 (pre-2014) to 106 (since 2014).

- Bharat's first Inland waterways terminal on River Ganga inaugurated.

- First of the 4 multi-modal terminals constructed on National Waterways – I

- Reduction in turnaround time at major ports over the last 4 years (94 hours in 2014 to 64 hours in 2017)

Putting Farmers First

Record Budgetary Allocation & Doubling Farmers' Income

- Rs 1,21,082 Cr (2009-14) to Rs 2,11,694 Cr (2014-19).

- Rs 1,290 Cr allocated under the National Bamboo Mission to set up small industries.

- Rs 2,000 Cr for Agri-Market infrastructure fund set up.

- Introduction of new crop insurance scheme to mitigate risks at an affordable cost.

- Provision of quality seeds and nutrients based on the soil health of each field..

Agricultural Production & Procurement Touched New High (2018-19)

- Food grains (283.37 MT), Rice (115.63 MT), Pulses (23.22 MT).

- Sugarcane (400.37 MT), Horticulture (314.87 MT), Cereals (43.33 MT).

- 64 Lakh metric tonnes of pulses and oil seeds were procured at MSP from farmers (2014-18).

- The extent of buffer stock of pulses increased from 1.5 lakh tonnes to 20 lakh tonnes.

Accelerated Growth

GST Empowering Business & Ease of Living

- GST provides relief of about Rs 80,000 Cr annually to consumers.

- Over 57.5 Lakh new taxpayers registered post GST (till Nov 2018).

- More than Rs 91,149 Cr GST refunds were disposed of.

- Significant decrease in transport times with elimination of check-posts.

Bold Reforms Fueling the Next Wave of Growth

- Historic Insolvency & Bankruptcy code leading to recovery of Rs 3 lakhs Cr by banks & creditors.

- Home buyer's dreams & rights are protected by Real Estate Regulation Act.

- Transparent resource allocation with 89 coal mines allocated.

- The Payment of Wages (Amendment) Act 2017 – empowering workers.

Ease of Doing Business & MSMEs

- Record jump in rankings (construction permits from 184 (2014) to 52 (2018).

- Getting electricity (137 in 2014 to 24 in 2018), Trading across borders (from 216 (2014) to 80 (2018).

- 12 new initiatives for growth of MSMEs (Easy credit, wider markets, better technology).

- Corporate tax rate slashed to 25% for companies with annual turnover up to 250 Cr from 50 Cr.

Women-Led Development

Facilitating the Well-Being of Expectant Mothers

- More than 1.8 Cr antenatal check-ups have been conducted (June 2018).

- More than 14,641 health facilities across all states/UT.

- Over 87 lakh poor pregnant women immunized.

- Paid maternity leave extended to 26 weeks (one of the highest durations in the world).

- Cash incentive of Rs 6000 to pregnant/lactating women.

From Women's Development to Women-Led Development

- The sex ratio at birth improved in 104 identified districts.

- Multiple scholarships for girl children's education & increase in girls' enrollment in secondary schools.

- Over 9 Cr women benefited from the Mudra & Standup India scheme.

- 8 Cr poor women got LPG connections.

- Cabinet approved enhancement of honorarium to Anganwadi workers benefiting 27 lakhs women.

Promoting Social Empowerment for Women

- Triple Talaq bill passed in Lok Sabha to empower Muslim women.

- Muslim women can now perform Haj without a male guardian.

- Over 10.5 Cr toilets built – ensuring the dignity of women.

- Provision of death penalty for rape of girl child under 12 years.

Commitment to Social Justice

Holistic Development of Divyangs

- Reservation for Divyang persons in Govt. jobs increased from 3% to 4%.

- Aids & assistive equipment worth Rs 700 Cr distributed to about 12 Lakh persons with disabilities.

- 1 Lakh health insurance covers people with autism, cerebral palsy, and many disabilities.

- All 34 international & 48 domestic airports and 644 railway stations have been provided with accessible features.

Fulfilling Aspirations Through Social Inclusion

- Strong amendments to the SC/ST Act

- Panchteerth: Paying tributes to Babasaheb Ambedkar by developing 5 places associated with his life.

- Historic budget allocation of Rs 1,26,887 Cr (2019) for SC/ST communities welfare.

- Over 5.7 Cr students benefited (2014-18) with scholarships worth Rs 15,918 Cr.

Empowering Through Education

- The stipend for day scholars increased from Rs 150 to Rs 225 & for hostelers from Rs 350 to Rs 525. Act.

- Free coaching for SC & OBC students (income eligibility raised from 4.5 Lakh to 6 lakh).

- For Pre-matric scholarships for OBCs, the rates of scholarship increased substantially.

Building a Health Bharat

Ensuring Quality & Affordable Healthcare

- 1387 medicines brought under price control regime, resulted in annual savings of Rs 5,066 Cr.

- Affordable medicines with PM Janaushadhi Kendras (5479 stores).

- The price of cardiac stents was reduced by 85%, & Knee implants were reduced by 69%.

- Ayushman Bharat – the world's largest Health Insurance initiative (up to 5 Lakh per family for 50 Cr people).

- Free Dialysis for poor & subsidized services to all patients (647 Dialysis Center across Bharat).

Eliminating Disease, One Dose at a Time

- Bharat validated the elimination of Maternal & Neonatal Tetanus in May 2015 (before the Global target of Dec 2015).

- Mission Indradhanush – covering 551 districts with 3.39 Cr children vaccinated.

- Treatment of drug-sensitive TB is provided through 4,00,000 DOT Centres.

- Inactivated Polio Vaccine (IPV) introduced in 2015, 6.4 Cr doses administered to children.

Policy for Healthy Bharat

- National Health Policy 2017 formulated after a gap of 15 years.

- Mental Healthcare Act – strengthens equality & equity in the provision of mental healthcare.

- Allied & Healthcare Professional Bill 2018 (benefited 8-9 lakh healthcare professionals).

Harnessing Yuva Shakti

Enabling Sports & Sportsmanship

- Financial assistance of Rs 5 lakh up to 8 years for talented players.

- The first Khelo India School Games launched in Jan 2018 (3507 players participated).

- National Sports University in Manipur.

- Bharat wins a historic 66 medals in the 2018 Commonwealth Games in Australia.

Transforming Education & Employment

- Numerous universities, 7 IITs, 7 IIMs, 14 hits, 2 IISER, 1 NIT, 103 KVs, 4 NID, 14 AIIMS, & 62 Navodaya. Vidyalayas established & have started functioning.

- Major reform in education by granting autonomy to quality institutes.

- Three prolonged approaches to employment creation (public sector, private sector & self-employment).

Skill Development & Training

- PM Skill Development Scheme (PMKVY) was launched to empower skills among youths.

- 25000 training Center across 633 trades & more than 1 Cr youngsters trained.

- Atal Innovation Mission – 8878 Atal Tinkering Labs in schools.

- To boost educational infrastructure in tribal areas, 463 Eklavya model residential schools.

Eliminating Corruption

Tribunals for Speedy Disposals of Cases

- Benami Property Transaction Act – Setting up appellate Tribunal & appointment of adjudicating authority.

- Rs 50,000 Cr confiscated in Benami Property Transaction Act.

- Fugitive Economic Offenders Bill Act – empower law enforcement to confiscate assets of economic offenders.

Enabling Legislations to Curb Corruption

- Clean auctions of coal blocks & telecom spectrum set a new benchmark.

- No more interviews for non-gazetted posts – merit-based candidates win.

- Time taken for environmental approvals reduced from 600 days to 180 days.

- Double taxation avoidance agreement with Mauritius, Cyprus & Singapore.

- Agreement of real-time information sharing with Switzerland.

Use of Technology to Boost Transparency

- Over Rs 7.66 Lakh Crore directly transferred into bank accounts of beneficiaries for 437 schemes.

- Aadhaar given legislative framework – More than 1 Cr income tax payees linked.

- GEM online platform for transparent public procurement – 20 lakh transactions worth Rs 33,050 Cr with 25% savings.

World Sees New Bharat

Bharat Becomes a Global Growth Engine

- Bharat has become the world's fastest-growing large economy.

- Bharat rated highly on all investments & macroeconomic indicators.

- Bharat's GDP increased by 31% between 2013 to 2017, while global GDP increased by 4%.

Bharat leading the World Toward Renewable Energy

- Bharat's stand in Global Renewable Energy Install Capacity (4th in Wind power, 5th in Solar power, 5th in renewable energy).

- Over USD $ 40 bn in green energy space in just 4 years.

- Renewable energy installed capacity increased from 35 GW (2014) to 80 GW (2019).

Bharat Leads the Fight Against Climate Change

- Bharat played a leading role at COP21 in Paris

- Bharat initiated the International Solar Alliance in 2018

- Govt approved resolution to open ISA membership to all UN member countries (121 countries participated)

Modi Government – Term 2 (2019 – 2024) – Delivered Development

The first term (2014 – 2019) of Prime Minister Shri. Narendra Modi delivered a strong **CHANGE** for Bharat. Bringing the Bharat economy from fragile 5, removing the country from the shadow of terrorism and preparing it for the decisive fight against the menace, resolving to rejuvenate farmers and poor in the true sense, and ability to turn challenges into opportunities were hallmarks of the first five- year tenure of Narendra Modi Government.

The nation strongly supported 2nd term of the Modi Government with great hope and trust. The huge mandate was given by the people of Bharat with "Great expectations."

Nation's Expectations

The nation felt confident that the 2nd term of the Modi govt would undertake bold reforms and demonstrate concrete action to push investments, increase growth, and create jobs.

As the Modi govt successfully secured its massive second consecutive term in office, the country welcomed this with great expectations for continued reforms. Govt. will continue strengthening the initiatives undertaken and boost their development agenda, thereby accelerating the entrepreneurial ecosystem and infrastructure development, etc. Furthermore, the government was expected to keep implementing its strategies in harnessing the potential transformative technologies to not only facilitate Bharat's economic growth and social development but also create employment opportunities for the youth of the country—a key vision of the Modi govt.

The nation felt positive that the government would continue its focus and provide support to the startup and fin-tech ecosystem in the country. Thanks to the overall Digital India program, there have been innumerable benefits that have driven the digital economy and led to fin-tech growth. Such initiatives are to be given impetus under the umbrella program of Digital India 2.0 and for a push toward financial inclusion and adoption of technology.

The industry's expectation was to give priority to propelling the Bharat economy, including enhancing investment expenditure, creating jobs through the private sector, addressing rural requirements, and continuing to keep the fiscal deficit under control. There was a hope that the Modi government would immediately start implementing more reforms like increasing liquidity in the financial sector, reducing the GST slabs, undertaking additional land and labor reforms, continuing major infrastructure projects, and encouraging more private sector investment in the economy".

Youth expected the Modi Govt to take forward the Digital India vision to the next level in the coming 5 years, aiming to record Bharat as at least in the top 10 list of digitally advanced nations. New favorable policies by the government will help startups flourish in our country. Vital steps have to be taken to educate people of all sections and inculcate habits of digitization through attractive incentives, underlining the ease of operability and strengthening the security around these systems. Modi govt was expected to create a secure, accessible, and innovative structure that will allow the Fintechs, Startups, and the digital payments industry to thrive at a booming rate while also taking measures to nurture innovation to keep up with this rapidly evolving sector.

I covered the 2nd term poll promises & the delivered development initiatives of PM Modi.

Nation First
Zero Tolerance Approach to Terrorism

Promised

- We will firmly continue our policy of 'Zero Tolerance' against terrorism and extremism and will continue to follow our policy of giving a free hand to our security forces in combating terrorism.

Delivered

The government, under the leadership of Prime Minister Shri Narendra Modi, has been working on 4 directive principles- to enable the country to deal with threats to its security & sovereignty; to take every action to protect national interests; to create safe conditions within the country to facilitate progress, improve the lives of the people & fulfill their aspirations and to build an environment with friendly countries to tackle global challenges such as terrorism unitedly.

- Global diplomatic initiatives: India hosted the third "No Money for Terror" conference, with 75 participating countries, to end international terrorism by cutting off their funding.

- As plenary chair for the year 2023, India strengthened its commitment toward the principles of the Wassenaar Arrangement, which promotes "transparency and greater responsibility in transfers of conventional arms and dual-use goods and technologies" to prevent destabilizing accumulations and to prevent the acquisition of these items by terrorists."

- As a member of the Financial Action Task Force (FATF), India's meticulous efforts forced Pakistan to place Dawood Ibrahim on the designated list of terrorists and attach some of his bank accounts and assets.

- Use of hard force: India's readiness "to strike militarily at terrorist camps by crossing the Line of Control of the International Boundary," which was proven in the aftermath of the Balakot strikes.

- MHA declared 4 organizations as 'Terrorist Organizations', 7 individuals as 'Terrorist,' and 3 organizations as 'Unlawful Associations' in 2023

National Security
Strengthening our Armed Forces

Promised

- Speed up the purchases of outstanding defense-related equipment and weapons to make them available to our Armed Forces.

- Take focused steps to strengthen the Armed Forces' strike capability.

Delivered

- Bharat's defense budget, for the first time in history, crossed Rs. 3,00,000 crores in 2019-20. By the year 2023-24, the defense budget grew to Rs 5.94 lakh crores.

- Bharat's Defense Acquisition Council in September 2023 approved nine proposals to buy defense equipment worth a combined 450 billion rupees ($5.41 billion) from domestic vendors.

- The Defense Acquisition Council, the top government body for capital acquisition approvals for the Indian military, approved the procurement of survey vessels for the navy, plus 12 Su-30 aircraft and Dhruvastra short-range air-to-surface missiles for the air force.

- The commissioning of Bharat's first indigenous aircraft carrier, INS Vikrant, by Prime Minister Modi.

Self-reliance in Defense Sector

Promised

Focus on 'Make in India in Defense' to enable indigenous production of defense equipment, generate employment, and attract private participation in the defense sector.

Delivered

- Defense production in India, in FY2022-23, crossed Rs. 1 lakh crores for the first time. This figure stood at around Rs. 95,000 crores in FY2021–22.

- Defense exports have crossed Rs 16,000 crores from a meager Rs 900 crore before 2014. The exports were expected to touch the Rs 20,000 crore mark in the financial year 2023-24. India now exports defense equipment to more than 85 countries.

- The General Electric (GE) Aerospace-Hindustan Aeronautics Limited deal to co-produce F-414 fighter jet engines in Bharat - India, the "fourth country to manufacture jet engines. Tejas aircraft will be fitted with these Made in India engines."

- Induction of the LCH (Light Combat Helicopter) 'Prachand,' designed and developed by Hindustan Aeronautics Limited (HAL), into the Indian Air Force

- The launch of frontline warships of the Indian Navy, 'Surat' and 'Udaygiri'. 'Surat' is the fourth Stealth-Guided Missile Destroyer of the P15B class. 'Udaygiri' is the second Stealth Frigate of the P17A class. These are the next-generation stealth-guided missile destroyers of the Indian Navy.

- **The** Raksha Mantri launched two frontline warships of the Indian Navy, 'Surat' and 'Udaygiri.' 'Surat' is the fourth Stealth-Guided Missile Destroyer of the P15B class (next-generation stealth-guided missile destroyers of the Indian Navy), while 'Udaygiri' is the second Stealth Frigate of the P17A class. 'Surat' was delivered to the Indian Navy in November 2022.

- 100 Indian firms are now involved in the manufacturing and export of defense equipment, including Dornier-228, 155 mm Advanced Towed Artillery Guns, Brahmos Missiles, Akash Missile System, radars, and simulators.

Welfare of Soldiers

Promised

We promise to create a more effective framework for the resettlement of our Armed Forces veterans.

Delivered

- A budgetary allocation for defense pension of Rs 28,138 Crores was made to meet the additional requirements for the revision of Armed Forces Pensioners/ Family Pensioners under One Rank One Pension (OROP).

- An impressive 52% increase was made for the Ex-Servicemen Contributory Health Scheme (ECHS) with BE allocation of Rs. 5431.56 Crore in FY 2023-24 to transform the healthcare outreach to the Armed Forces veterans. The enhancement will ensure 'Cashless Health Services' and improved 'Service Delivery' to our veterans and their dependents across India.

- The payment received from the Agniveer Corpus Fund by the Agniveers enrolled in the Agnipath Scheme 2022 proposed to be exempt from taxes.

- Self-employment schemes offered to ex-servicemen under the Directorate General Resettlement (DGR) now include industries that make genuine contributions to the country's industrial productivity.

- More hospitals and polyclinics have now been brought under the Ex-servicemen Contributory Health Scheme (ECHS). As of February 2023, 427 polyclinics now provide cashless medical treatment to veterans and their dependents in 30 regional centers all over the country.

Modernization of Police Forces

Promised

- Modernize the Central Armed Police Forces to make them more effective in combating internal security challenges.

- Provide assistance to the states to upgrade their police forces through the 'Scheme for Modernization of Police Forces'

Delivered

- Under the Modernization of Police Forces (MPF), a total central financial outlay of Rs.26,275 crore is allocated for the period 2021-22 to 2025-26 to strengthen the criminal justice system further. The scheme includes plans to develop operationally independent high-quality forensic sciences facilities in states/Union Territories and to make the police force sensitive and trained in emerging technologies.

- The Modernization of Police Forces (MPF) scheme categorizes the states into two groups - Category 'A' [North & North-East States) and Category 'B' [the remaining states]. Category A states are eligible to receive 90% of financial assistance from the Center. The Category B states receive 60 percent of their funding from the Center under the MPF scheme.

- A central outlay of Rs.18,839 crore was allocated for security-related expenditure for the Union Territories of Jammu & Kashmir, insurgency-affected North Eastern states, and affected areas affected by Left-Wing Extremism (LWE).

- Six LWE-related schemes with a Central outlay of Rs.8,689 crore have been approved, including schemes that cover the Most LWE-Affected Districts & Districts of Concern.

Combating Infiltration

Promised

- To expeditiously complete the National Register of Citizens process in high-infiltration areas on a priority basis and in a phased manner in other parts of the country.

- To take steps to prevent illegal immigration in the Northeastern states by strengthening the border security and with Smart Fencing.

Delivered

- A cabinet note and a bill moved by the Union Home Ministry in the year 2022 proposed the setting up of a national database of all Indian citizens and registering the births and deaths of all citizens at the national level. This is being viewed as the first step toward the setting up of a nationwide NRC. (Assam & Manipur state to implement NRC)

- Smart Fences with advanced sensor and CCTV camera technologies have been installed along the Line of Control along our northern borders to prevent infiltration attempts. & these smart fences use state-of-the-art sensors and CCTV cameras that pick up the slightest movement to immediately alert the control center, making it difficult for the infiltrators to get inside the country

Reinforcing Border Security

Promised

- We will focus on the creation of developmental and other necessary infrastructure in border areas to ensure that border security is strengthened.

- Six integrated checkposts were completed to facilitate easier trade and travel between us and our neighboring countries; 14 more by 2024. On completion, all trade movements shall be carried out through these integrated checkposts.

Delivered

- Other regular actions, including round-the-clock nakas at strategic points, group security in the form of static guards, and intensified Cordon and Search Operations (CASO), have brought down the casualties among our Armed Forces from 91 in 2018 to 25 as of November 30, 2023.

- India shares a land border of over 1643 km with Myanmar via 4 northeastern states. A 100-km-long smart fencing project along the Indo-Myanmar is in the pipeline to prevent ethnic violence and insurgencies in these border states.

Coastal Safety

Promised

- Establish coastal police stations.

- Establish National Committee for Strengthening Maritime & Coastal Security, Island Information System, and National Academy of Coastal Policing

Delivered

India is the 7th largest fishing Nation in the world. Around 95 percent of India's trade by volume and 70 percent by value is carried through the sea routes and an Exclusive Economic Zone (EEZ) of about 2.37 million sq. km. There are presently 12 major ports and 200 notified minor and intermediate ports in India.

- Under the Coastal Security Scheme, 204 Coastal Police Stations have been operationalized.

- Two hundred 4 boats, 36 jetties, 284 four-wheelers, 554 two-wheelers, 97 checkposts, 58 out-posts, and 30 barracks, and navigation/communication equipment, detection equipment, card readers, equipment enhancing night operation capabilities of boats have been provided to the coastal states/UTs.

- The country's first National Maritime Security Coordinator (NMSC) was appointed in the year 2022 to "ensure cooperation and harmonized functioning between the various agencies and stakeholders tasked to ensure the protection of India's vast coastline and safeguard interests in the Exclusive Economic Zone."

- In addition to terror attacks, emphasis is also being given to non-traditional challenges, such as human trafficking, illegal fishing, climate-induced crises, and maritime pollution along the coast. The Indian Navy and Indian Coast Guard, along with the state marine police, are building the security infrastructure, including Coastal Security Schemes, which involve the MoD, Ministry of Home Affairs (MHA), coastal states & union territories.

Citizenship Amendment Bill

Promised

- Protect individuals of religious minority communities from neighboring countries escaping persecution.

- Clear the misunderstandings about the Bill among the sections of the population from the Northeastern states.

- Give Indian citizenship to Hindus, Jains, Buddhists, Sikhs, and Christians escaping persecution from India's neighboring countries.

Delivered

The Citizenship (Amendment) Act 2019 (CAA) was passed by the Parliament of India on 11 December 2019. It amended the Citizenship Act of 1955 by providing an accelerated pathway to Indian citizenship for persecuted religious minorities from Afghanistan, Bangladesh, and Pakistan who are Hindus, Sikhs, Buddhists, Jains, Parsis, or Christians and arrived in India before the end of December 2014. The act came into force on 10 January 2020

Combating Left-Wing Extremism

Promised

- Take effective steps against left-wing extremism and eliminate it in the next 5 years.

- Further develop economic and social infrastructure such as roads, mobile towers, schools, and medical facilities in the tribal areas affected by left-wing extremism.

Delivered

- Incidents in Naxal-affected states have come down by 77% in 2022 in comparison to the high of 2010 & LWE will be eliminated by 2025 as per Govt.

- 17,679 LWE-related incidents and 6,984 deaths between 2004 and 2014. But 7,649 LWE-related incidents and 2,020 deaths from 2014 to 2023 (till 15 June 23).

- 704 Fortified Police Stations (FPS) have been sanctioned for LWE-affected states with an estimated cost of Rs. 1554 crores, of which 603 have been constructed.

- The expansion of the road network, consisting of 1,630 km of roads and 75 bridges, was completed in 2023.

- Under the Skill Development Scheme for LWE-affected 47 districts, 3 ITIs & 11 Skill Development Centres (SDCs) have been made functional.

- The decision has been made to open 15 bank branches and 2344 post offices to cover 6799 uncovered villages in LWE-affected districts for financial inclusion in these areas.

- Funds are released under Special Central Assistance (SCA) to the most affected LWE districts to fill critical gaps in public infrastructure and services. Rs. 323.45 crore have been released in 2023.

Jammu & Kashmir Article 370

Promised

- Annulment of the discriminatory Article 35A of the Constitution of India

- Ensure a safe and peaceful environment for all residents of the state.

- The safe return of Kashmiri Pandits

- Financial assistance for the resettlement of refugees from West Pakistan, Pakistan-occupied-Jammu and Kashmir (POJK) and Chhamb.

Delivered

- Article 370 & 35A was scrapped in 2019 by Modi govt to bring One Nation, One Law & One head of the nation, whereby all the provisions of the Indian Constitution were made to apply to the state after 70 years.

- The state of Jammu & Kashmir was restructured into 2 union territories: Jammu and Kashmir and Ladakh.

- During 2021-22, Rs. 34704. crore was allocated to the Union Territory of Jammu and Kashmir as Grants-in-aid and Rs. 5958 crores has been allocated to the UT of Ladakh. During 2022-23, Rs. 35,581 crores were allocated to the Union Territory of Jammu and Kashmir as Grants-in-aid and Rs. 5958 crores were allocated to the UT of Ladakh.

- Under the West Pakistan Refugees (WPR) scheme, financial assistance of Rs.5.5 lakh per family is disbursed to all WPR families (more than 1640 families benefited)

Doubling Farmers' Income

Welfare of Farmers

Promised

- Pradhan Mantri Kisan Samman Nidhi Yojana to all

- Pension for small and marginal farmers

- Rs 25 lakh crore investment in Agri-rural sector

- Interest-free Kisan Credit Card loans

- Voluntary enrollment in Pradhan Mantri Fasal Bima.

- Empowering Farmers through Policies.

- Assurance of Quality Seeds

Delivered

- PM Modi released the 15th installment of the PM KISAN scheme on 15th November 2023. Under the scheme, an income support of 6,000/- per year in 3 equal installments will be provided to all land-holding poor farmer families.

- The funds are transferred directly to the beneficiary's account.

- In 2022-23, a total amount of Rs. 58,201 crores was disbursed to eligible beneficiaries.

- Launched on August 09, 2019, the Pradhan Mantri Kisan Maan-Dhan Yojana (PM-KMY) is a contributory and voluntary old-age pension scheme for all land-holding Small and Marginal Farmers (SMFs). The entry age for the scheme is between 18 to 40 years.

- Under the leadership of PM Modi (June 2020), approval was given for the setting up of Project Development Cells (PDCs) in Ministries/Departments of the Government of Bharat to attract investments in Bharat.

- Agriculture Infrastructure Fund (AIF) - Rs. 1 Lakh Crore will be provided by banks and financial institutions as loans.

- Institutional Credit to the Agricultural Sector continued to grow to 18.6 lakh crore in 2021-22

- Kisan Credit Card Scheme - Loans of up to Rs.3 lakh and produce marketing loans are available under this scheme. Credit is available for a period of up to 3 years, and repayment can be made once the harvest season is over.

- Insurance coverage for KCC scheme holders up to Rs.50,000 in the case of permanent disability or death

- The comprehensive crop insurance scheme is compulsory for farmers who have borrowed loans from financial institutions and optional for farmers who have not sought financial assistance.

- As a result of various pathbreaking initiatives by Modi govt, Bharat was among the top 10 global agri exporters. According to the WTO's Trade Statistical Review (2022), India's agricultural exports and imports share in the world's agriculture trade in 2021 were 2.4% and 1.7%, respectively.

- One hundred sixty-one state seed testing laboratories and six central seed testing Laboratories are functioning in the country now.

- The National Bureau of Plant Genetic Resources (NBPGR) has conserved 94,609 native Indian varieties of different crops and trees in Gene Banks located in different states.

- The Protection of Plant Varieties and Farmer's Rights Authority (PPV & FRA) has registered 1896 native Indian varieties of different crops, enabling both the preservation of these seeds and the farmer to commercialize these varieties.

- The Indian Council of Agricultural Research (ICAR) - In the last 7 years, in 1956, improved varieties have been developed, out of which 924 were cereals, 291 oilseeds, and 304 pulses. Two hundred 88 varieties of horticultural crops have also been developed.

Development of Agri- Allied Sectors

Promised

- Oilseeds Mission - Self-sufficiency in oil seeds and other agriproducts.

- Warehouse Network across the Country

- Promote chemical-free organic farming in an additional 20 lakh hectares of hilly, tribal, and rainfed areas in the next 5 years.

- Launch a dedicated e-commerce portal to enhance the availability of organic produce to the doorsteps of consumers.

- Goshalas in the country will be linked to the promotion of organic farming.

- Promotion of organic eco-tourism in the vicinity of organic farming will also ensure additional income to the farmers.

- National Beekeeping and Honey Mission

Delivered

- The constitution of the National Mission on Edible Oils - Oil Palm (NMEO-OP) and the National Mission on Oilseeds and

Oil Palm (NMOOP). With vegetable oil being the No. 1 item on the import list, the emphasis is on scaling up the oil palm area, according to the NMEO-OP. The agency is working with the objective to increase the area of oil palm from 3.5 lakh hectares in 2019-20 to 10 lakh hectares by 2025-26 and to increase crude palm oil production from 0.27 lakh tonnes during 2019-20 to 11.20 lakh tonnes by 2025-26.

- The Pradhan Mantri Kisan SAMPADA Yojana (Scheme for Agro-Marine Processing and Development of Agro-Processing Clusters) – A total of 96 food processing projects have been approved & and a total of 47.52 lakh farmers have benefited across the country. PMKSY has assisted in generating total employment (direct and indirect) of 13.09 lakh.

- Paramparagat Krishi Vikas Yojana (PKVY) – The scheme supports cluster formation, training, certification and marketing. Financial assistance of Rs. 50,000 per hectare is provided for 3 years, out of which 62 percent (Rs. 31,000) is given as an incentive to farmers for organic inputs.

- Mission Organic Value Chain Development for North Eastern Region (MOVCDNER) - The scheme promotes third-party certified organic farming of niche crops of the northeast region through Farmer Producer Organizations (FPOs), with a focus on exports.

- The organic e-commerce platform www.jaivikkheti.in is being strengthened to link farmers directly with retail as well as bulk buyers.

- The government initiated public-private partnership (PPP) models to bring in the initial capital investment to Gaushalas.

- "Eco Circuit" was identified as one of the 15 thematic circuits under the Swadesh Darshan Scheme to promote Eco-Tourism in the country.

- Rs. 500 crores allocated for the National Beekeeping & Honey Mission (NBHM) for 3 years (2020-21 to 2022-23) as part of the "Sweet Revolution" and the Atma Nirbhar Bharat scheme.

- 10,000 Beekeepers/Beekeeping & Honey Societies/Firms/ Companies with 16.00lakhs honeybee colonies have been registered with the National Bee Board [NBB].

- Honey production has increased from 76,150 MTs (2013-14) to 1,20,000 MTs (2019-20) which is a 57.58 % increase.

- The export of honey has increased from 28,378.42 MTs (2013-14) to 59536.74 MTs (2019-20), which is a 109.80 % increase.

Expanding Irrigation in Mission Mode

Promised

- Complete 68 irrigation projects under the Pradhan Mantri Krishi Sinchai Yojana.

- Further, expand the Pradhan Mantri Krishi Sinchai Yojana to realize 100% irrigation potential of the country

- Bring one crore hectares of agricultural land under micro-irrigation.

Delivered

- There is a new irrigation potential of 24.35 lakh hectares under the Accelerated Irrigation Benefit Program.

- Seventy-eight lakh hectares have been covered under the "More Crop per Drop" micro-irrigation scheme.

- Further, in December 2021, the implementation of PMKSY for the period 2021-22 to 2025-26 was approved by the government.

- So far, under PMKSY, Rs 49,750 Cr fund assistance has been provided by the Modi govt.

Cooperatives

Promised

- Enable the creation of 10,000 new Farmer Producer Organizations (FPOs) by 2022.

Delivered

The concept behind Farmer Producer Organizations is that farmers, who are the producers of agricultural products, can form groups and register themselves under the Indian Companies Act.

- Modi govt. allowed the formation of 1100 New Farmer Producer Organizations (FPOs) in the Cooperative Sector.

- Under the FPO Scheme, financial assistance of Rs. 33 lakhs is provided to each FPO. Further, financial assistance of Rs. 25 lakhs per FPO is provided to the Cluster-Based Business Organizations.

- As of 30th June 2023, 10,000 FPOs have been allocated to various Implementing Agencies (IAs), out of which 6319 FPOs have been registered across the country.

- All India Agri Transport Call Centre launched (2020) & e-NAM.

Convergence of Agriculture and Technology

Promised

- **Develop and launch apps for renting or custom hiring agricultural equipment.**

- Use technology to keep the farmers better informed about the prices of their products.

- Encourage young agri-scientists to utilize technologies.

- Solar energy is an additional source of income for farmers and will encourage solar farming.

- Digitization of Land Records

- Establish a network of mobile veterinary dispensaries to provide doorstep service to farmers.

- Expand the coverage of immunization and eliminate Foot and Mouth Disease and Brucellosis

- Launch a National Feed and Fodder Mission to eliminate the shortage of fodder.

Delivered

- There are more than 38,000 Custom Hiring Centers (CHCs) all over the country launched by Modi Govt. These CHCs currently rent out 250,000 pieces of farm equipment every year.

- The application is also to help promote new technology like Happy Seeder, which aims to prevent stubble burning that causes air pollution.

- Several apps, developed both by the government and private parties, are now available for free that inform the farmers of the prices and demands for their agricultural produces

- Modi govt. has established 22 Precision Farming Development Centers (PFDCs) throughout the country to focus on high-tech agriculture practices, including micro-irrigation, vertical farming, hydroponics, aeroponics, protected cultivation, and plasticulture

- The world's biggest solar installation, Bhadla Solar Park, is in the North Indian state of Rajasthan, with an installed capacity of 2245 MW – enough to power 4.5 million homes

- Agriculture Voltage Technology - This technology can increase farmers' incomes by generating electricity and growing cash crops simultaneously on the same piece of land.

- Digital India Land Records Modernization Program (DILRMP) launched with 100% funding by the Center, which allocates a 14-digit alphanumeric Unique Land Parcel Identification Number (ULPIN)

- The Records of Rights have been transliterated in all the 22 scheduled languages, with 94% of the digitization targets having already been achieved.

- The Animal Mobile Medical Ambulances scheme funded to all states & UTs can be utilized by calling the toll-free number "1962".

- The National Animal Disease Control Program (NADCP) is being implemented to control Foot & Mouth Disease and Brucellosis by completely vaccinating cattle, buffalo, sheep, and goats.

- The Technology Development Board (TDB), operating under the Department of Science & Technology (DST), launched the project titled "Commercialization and Manufacturing of Bio-Trace Minerals used in Feed for Animals"

Fisheries – Blue Revolution

Promised

- Launch' Matsya Sampada Yojana' with an allocation of Rs. 10,000 crores to build storage and marketing resources for small and traditional fishermen

- Promote aquaculture through easy access to credit.

- Facilitate the farming of seaweed, pearl, and ornamental fish.

- Welfare Programmes for all Fishermen

Delivered

- Pradhan Mantri Matsya Sampaday Yojana (PMMSY) was launched with a historic investment of Rs. 20,050 crores to be implemented over a period of 5 years from FY 2020-21 to FY 2024-25.

- Sixty-seven minor fishing harbors and 7 major fishing harbors have been commissioned.

- In 2022, India's seafood exports reached a record high of USD $7.08 billion.

- Due to various initiatives by Govt, the aquaculture industry has been growing at an average annual rate of 8%.

- Under the Pradhan Mantri Matsya Sampada scheme, the government pays for half the cost of setting up a pond for pearl fishing, and as of 2022, the Department for Fisheries has given financial support to 232 pearl farming ponds.

- Under the Pradhan Mantri Matsya Sampada Yojana (PMMSY), for the welfare of the fishermen, a sum of Rs.4500 for the fishers' families during the fishing ban/lean period.

- The insurance coverage is Rs.5,00,000/- against accidental death or permanent total disability; Rs.2,50,000/- for permanent partial disability; and insurance coverage for hospitalization expenses in the event of an accident for a sum of Rs. 25,000.

On the Path of Gram Swaraj

Promised

- Ensure a pucca house for every family who is living in a kutcha house by 2022

- Launch' Jal Jivan Mission' to ensure piped water connection to every household by 2024

- Ensure that every Gram Panchayat is connected through a high-speed optical fiber network by 2022

- Launch a massive 'Rural Road Upgradation Program' to connect centers of education, healthcare centers, and markets with hinterlands to promote rural growth.

- Ensure 100% disposal of liquid wastewater and reuse of wastewater.

Delivered

- Against the mandated target of construction of 2.95 crore rural houses under PMAY-G, Modi govt sanctioned 2.94 crore rural houses to the beneficiaries, and 2.54 crore rural houses have already been completed.

- Under the 'Jal Jeevan Mission Program, rural tap water connections increased from 16.64% in 2019 to 62.84% within a span of 41 months (3 Crore connections to 13 Crore connections)

- A total of 2,50,000 GPs (2,07,230 GPs on OFC and 4,351 GPs on satellite) have been made Service Ready in the country.

- Wi-Fi hotspots have been installed in 1,04,674 GPs.

- 6,01,026 Fiber to the Home broadband connections are provided.

- A massive 7.44 lakh km of rural roads were completed on a mission mode under the Rural Road Development Scheme (PMGSY)

- An ODF Plus village is one that has sustained its Open Defecation Free (ODF) status along with implementing either solid or liquid waste management systems.

- The country has achieved yet another major milestone under the Swachh Bharat Mission (Grameen) Phase II. 75% of villages (4.43 lakh) achieved ODF Plus status under Phase II of the Mission.

India as the world's 3ʳᵈ Largest Economy

Roadmap for 5 trillion dollar Economy & Tax Policy

Promised

- Make India the third-largest economy in the world by 2030.

- Make India a US$ 5 trillion economy by 2025 and a US$ 10 trillion economy by 2032

- Lowering the taxes

Delivered

- Bharat economy witnessed rapid growth under the visionary leadership of Prime Minister Shri Narendra Modi. Between 2014 and 2023, Bharat rose from its position as the 11th to the fifth (largest) economy in the world.

- According to the IMF's World Economic Outlook, the size of the Indian economy will increase from $3.2 trillion in 2021-22 to $3.5 trillion in 2022-23 and cross $5 trillion in 2026-27.

- The Union Budget 2023 raised the minimum taxable income to Rs. 3,00,000 from the previous Rs 2,50,000 minimum amount

Goods and Service Tax & 100 Lakh Crore Investment

Promised

- Simplify the Goods and Service Tax.

- Capital investment of Rs.100 lakh crore in the infrastructure sector by 2024

Delivered

- GST Council recommends (Oct 2023) NIL rate for food preparation of millet flour in powder form and containing at least 70%

- GST Council recommends reducing GST on molasses from 28% to 5% in relief to cane farmers for faster clearance of dues and to reduce the cost of manufacturing cattle feed.

- To promote tourism, the GST Council recommends conditional and limited duration IGST exemption to foreign flag foreign going vessels (converting to coastal run)

- National Infrastructure Pipeline (NIP) was launched with 6,835 projects and has expanded to capture over 9,288 projects with a total outlay of Rs 108.88 lakh crore between 2020-25

Make In India

Promised

- Top 50 Ranking in Ease of Doing Business Index – Take India's ranking into the top 50.

- Strengthening Companies Act by bringing about crucial amendments to make the Act more effective.

- Announce a New Industrial Policy 4.0 to gear up for technologies like artificial intelligence and electric mobility. Special efforts will be made for MSMEs.

- Network Approach for Growth – Develop clusters/networks with a special focus on Small and Medium Enterprises.

Delivered

- Pro-business reforms unleashed by Prime Minister Narendra Modi in the last 9 years are laying a strong foundation for New Bharat, easing the ease of doing business from 142 in 2014 to 63 in 2022, as per the World Bank.

- In 2020, the Govt passed the Companies (Amendment) Bill 2020 to further amend the Companies Act and decriminalize various compoundable offenses as well as promote ease of doing business in the country. Relaxation in corporate social responsibility (CSR) compliance requirements and the creation of separate benches at the National Company Law Appellate Tribunal (NCLAT) are among the proposed amendments.

- Govt has implemented AI & ML on its robust Single Window System' Champions,' which was launched by the Prime Minister on 1st June 2020. This is helping the MSMEs to manufacture essential and enabling products like sensors, motors, computer displays, and other animation technologies.

- Modi govt adopted the cluster development approach as a key strategy for enhancing the productivity and competitiveness as well as capacity building of Micro and Small Enterprises (MSMEs) and their collectives in the country.

Micro, Small and Medium Enterprises

Promised

- Achieve credit, under the Credit Guarantee Scheme of the Government of Bharat, from Rs.19,000 crore in 2017-18 to Rs.1,00,000 crore by 2024.

- Set up more than 150 Technology Centers by 2024 to mentor the skilling and prototyping of MSMEs.

- Provide focused and high-level skilling to more than 6 lakh people per year.

- Establish a National Traders' Welfare Board and create a National Policy for Retail Trade for the growth of retail businesses.

- Provide accident insurance of Rs. 10 lakhs to all the traders registered under GST.

- Along the lines of the Kisan credit card, create a scheme to give merchant credit cards to registered merchants.

Delivered

- Govt announced that the revamped credit guarantee scheme for MSMEs, proposed in the previous Budget, enables additional collateral-free guaranteed credit of ₹ 2 lakh crore.

- Keeping in view the success of the existing 18 Training Centers in serving MSMEs under the Technology Centre Systems Program (TCSP), 15 new Technology Centers are being established across the country as of August 2023.

- The technology centers all over the country offer more than 3100 programs connected to various kinds of MSMEs

- The first meeting of the National Traders' Welfare Board (NTWB) was held on 5 December 2023 in New Delhi.

- The National Trade Retail Policy is currently in advanced stages of finalization. When completed, the policy shall focus on ease of doing business, simplifying the licensing process, reducing compliance burden, and enabling the female workforce to work for longer hours, among others. A national portal is also being envisaged.

- Keeping in view the interests of small traders, the government launched a new pension scheme for them. **'National Traders Welfare Board'** will be constituted shortly, and **'National Retail Trade Policy'** will be formulated to promote retail business. Accident insurance of up to Rs. 10 lakh will also be provided to all traders registered under GST.

- Govt is planning to roll out a merchant credit card (MCC) facility for traders in the micro, small and medium enterprises (MSME) category this year.

Entrepreneurship & Startups

Promised

- Provide collateral-free credit up to Rs. 50 lakhs for entrepreneurs.

- 50% guarantee on the loan amount for female entrepreneurs and 25% of the loan amount for male entrepreneurs.

- Easing regulatory requirements for startups.

- Targeting time spent for tax compliance at an hour per month

- Facilitating the establishment of 50,000 new Startups in the nation by 2024

- Creating100 Innovation Zones in Urban Local Bodies

- Setting up 500 new incubators and accelerators by 2024

- Initiating ranking of Central Ministries, Departments, State Governments, and CPSUs for their increased engagement with startups

- Creation of a 'Seed Startup Fund' of ₹20,000 crores

- Support entrepreneurial ventures started by individuals from SC, ST & OBC as part of the 'Stand-up India' initiative.

- Set up a new 'Entrepreneurial Northeast' scheme.

Delivered

- Modi govt established the Credit Guarantee Scheme for Startups (CGSS) to provide credit guarantees to loans extended by Scheduled Commercial Banks, NBFCs, and the Securities and Exchange Board of India (SEBI).

- With effect from 01.04.2023, the credit limit for Guarantee Coverage under the Credit Guarantee Scheme for Micro &

Small Enterprises has been enhanced from ₹ 2 crore to ₹ 5 crore, and the annual guarantee fees have been reduced by 50%

- Over 50 regulatory reforms have been undertaken by the government since 2016 to enhance the ease of doing business, ease of raising capital, and reduce the compliance burden for the startup ecosystem.

- The government's Startup India flagship initiative has recognized 118,923 startups and has created 8.6 lakh jobs.

- The 100 Innovation Zones shall be linked to the Smart City Mission. The 100 cities shall house one innovation center each.

- IIT Madras' Centre for Research on Startups launches India's first information platform on Incubators & Accelerators (1,000 active incubators).

- The Fund of Funds Scheme (FFS) for startups commits Rs. 7,980 crores to 99 Alternative Investment Funds (AIFs) and Rs. 3,400 crores to 72 AIFs, which have in turn made investments of Rs. 14,077 crore in 791 startups.

- The National SC-ST Hub (NSSH) has been set up to provide professional support to entrepreneurs belonging to the Scheduled Castes and the Scheduled Tribes.

- Northeast India is home to over 900 DPIIT-recognized startups that have created over 8,800 job opportunities altogether. 42% of these startups have at least one female director.

- The North East Venture Fund (NEVF), the first dedicated Venture Fund for NE, has approved investments worth Rs 59.52 Crore in 29 ventures across sectors.

Using Tourism to Cluster Services

Promised

- Identify new and specific places of cultural or natural importance in order to develop them as comprehensive destinations.

- All UNESCO heritage sites in India will be upgraded to international-level facilities.

- The North Eastern states, island & coastal areas, and places of cultural importance will be developed while maintaining their unique heritage and ecosystem.

Delivered

- Modi govt launched its 'Swadesh Darshan' scheme with the objective of integrating the development of tourism under identified thematic circuits and sanctioned 76 projects in the country under different themes, including Eco Circuit.

- The Ministry of Tourism, under its 'National Mission on Pilgrimage Rejuvenation and Spiritual, Heritage Augmentation Drive (PRASHAD)' scheme, has also sanctioned 46 projects in the country.

- Govt's newly revamped Swadesh Darshan 2.0 (SD2.0) has identified 55 destinations for development under SD2.0. Eco-tourism is also one of the major themes identified under SD2.0.

- There are 3,696 centrally protected monuments/sites under the jurisdiction of the Archaeological Survey of India (ASI). Currently, India has 40 sites on the UNESCO World Heritage List and 52 sites (including 6 added in the year 2022) on the UNESCO Tentative List.

Transparent Economy

Promised

- Continue crackdown on Benami properties and illegal foreign bank accounts.

- Bring fugitive economic offenders back to India and prosecute them for their crimes.

Delivered

- Reforms were brought about to the laws governing benami transactions. The laws are now empowered to provisional attachment and subsequent confiscation of benami properties.

- India has geolocated more than 184 criminals in various countries and initiated formal proceedings for their return, reflecting increased leveraging of Interpol channels and relationships with law enforcement agencies internationally.

- Through continuous, coordinated efforts with Interpol, Bharat has managed to bring back 24 fugitives from abroad in 2023.

International Trade

Promised

- Ensure faster customs clearance of international cargo by relaxing clearance procedures, introducing self-declaration, etc, and adopting new scanning technology.

- Provide adequate financial and institutional support for exporters and export organizations.

Delivered

- RATIONALIZATION OF NUMBER OF BASIC CUSTOMS DUTY RATES: The number of basic customs duty rates on goods other than textiles and agriculture was reduced to 13 from 21.

- CENTRAL REPOSITORY FOR ALL NON-TARIFF MEASURES (NTMS) - a mechanism based on the globally accepted UNCTAD methodology for issuance of a Centralized Control Number (CCN) for mapping NTMS issued by all PGA.

- 24x7 custom clearance facility is available at 20 seaports and 17 airports.

- Launch of ICEGATE 2.0 – Ease of doing business monitoring dashboard of Indian customs, helping the public witness daily custom clearance time of import & export at all major customs stations.

- Launch of ICETRAK – A one-stop application for enabling custom clearances paperless and contactless.

- Launch of ICETRACK – Mobile application allows trade stakeholders to live track all status.

Infrastructure

Foundation for New India

Promised

- Create next-generation infrastructure, which will include gas grids and water grids, i-ways, regional airports, and wayside amenities along National highways.

- Continue public-private participation and efficient ground-level management on building infrastructure further to improve the quality of life and enhance the ease of living.

- Create a large number of jobs and livelihood opportunities.

Delivered

- At present, there is about a 17,000 km long natural gas pipeline network that is operational in the country. There are plans to develop additional pipelines of about 15,500 km to complete the National Gas Grid, and the same are at various stages of development.

- Under the National Perspective Plan (NPP) for Water Resources Development, a total of 30 river link projects have been identified: 14 link projects under the Himalayan Rivers Development Component and 16 link projects under the Peninsular Rivers Development Component. The National Water Development Agency (NWDA) has been entrusted with the work of the Interlinking of Rivers under the NPP. Out of 30 identified link projects under the NPP, the Pre-Feasibility Reports (PFRs) of all 30 links have been completed.

- Peninsular Rivers Development Component: The scheme is divided into 4 major parts - Interlinking of Mahanadi-Godavari-Krishna-Pennar-Cauvery rivers; interlinking of west flowing rivers, north of Bombay and south of Tapi; interlinking of Ken-Chambal; and diversion of other west flowing rivers.

- In October 2023, India had 149 operational airports for civil aviation, including 30 international, 12 customs, 107 domestic, and a few more civil aviation enclaves within military air bases.

- Modi Government has approved the 'revival of unserved and under-served airports' scheme for the revival and development of 100 unserved and under-served Airports, Helipads, and Water Aerodromes by 2024.

- Close to 2000 PPP (Public-Private Partnership) projects in various stages of implementation, Bharat's program is one of the largest in the world (as per World Bank).

- Employment in the major Industries related to the infrastructure sector has increased during 2022-23 as compared to 2020-21. In the manufacturing sector, the percentage of workers has increased to 11.4% in 2022-23 as compared to 10.9% in 2020-21

- As per the fourth round of QES (January-March 2022), the estimated total employment in the 9 selected sectors was 3.18 crore as compared to 2.37 crore in the sixth Economic Census (2013-14)

Ensuring Urban Development

Promised

- Ensure growth of suburban townships through infrastructure development.

- Set up 5 regional centers of excellence on urban issues.

- Urban Mobility - Provide technology-based urban mobility solutions, increase the use of public transport, and enhance walkability and cycle use.

- Promote a common mobility card/ticketing across different modes of transport.

- Ensure that 50 cities are covered with a strong metro network.

Delivered

- Four greenfield industrial cities or nodes are being developed in Gujarat, Maharashtra, Uttar Pradesh, and Madhya Pradesh under the Delhi-Mumbai Industrial Corridor (DMIC).

- Modi Govt has officially designated four institutions throughout the country as Centers of Excellence (CoE) for urban planning and design – Centre for Environment Planning & Technology (CEPT) University in Ahmedabad; Indian Institute of Technology (IIT) Kharagpur, West Bengal; School of Planning and Architecture (SPA) Delhi; and the National Institute of Technology (NIT) Calicut.

- These institutes are set to receive a grant of INR 250 crore (INR 2.5 Billion) to be used toward the development and training of Bharat-specific knowledge in Urban Planning and Design over the next 25 years.

- Rail-based Mass Rapid Transport Systems (MRTS), Light Rail Transport Systems (Metrolite), Bus Rapid Transport Systems (BRTS), and Electric vehicles (EV) are part of the government initiatives.

- National Common Mobility Card (NCMC) is a single smart card enabling commuters to book tickets, use it for metro, buses, and trains, and pay for toll and parking.

- Bharat's metro network is the 3rd largest in the world, with 895 km of metro lines operational in 20 different cities. PM-e-bus Sewa scheme with 10,000 e-Buses deployed on a PPP model in 169 cities.

Swachh Bharat Mission

Promised

- Sustainable Solid Waste Management in every village

- Ensure that all habitations attain open defecation free status, and those that have attained the status sustain the behavioral change.

Delivered

- An ODF Plus village is one that has sustained its Open Defecation Free (ODF) status along with implementing either solid or liquid waste management systems.

- The country has achieved yet another major milestone under the Swachh Bharat Mission (Grameen) Phase II. 75% of villages (4.43 lakh) achieving ODF Plus status under Phase II of the Mission

Jal Shakti

Promised

- Form a new Ministry of Water for holistic water management and implement ambitious programs like river-water linking.

- Launch' Jal Jivan Mission' to implement 'Nal se Jal' to ensure piped water for every household by 2024.

- Ensuring sustainability of water supply through a special focus on the conservation of rural water bodies and groundwater recharge

Delivered

- The Ministry of Jal Shakti was established in May 2019. Two ministries, namely the Ministry of Water Resources, River Development & Ganga Rejuvenation, and the Ministry of Drinking Water and Sanitation, were merged together to form the Ministry of Jal Shakti.

- United Nations Sustainable Development Goal (SDG) 6.1 aims to achieve universal and equitable access to safe and affordable drinking water for all by 2030. The Jal Jeevan Mission (JJM)-Har Ghar Jal is being implemented by the Government of Bharat in partnership with states/UTs to make provision for tap water supply to every rural household of the country by 2024, much earlier than 2030- the SDG 6.1 global timeline.

- Out of 19.4 Crore rural households in the country, provision of tap water supply has been made to 14.13 Crore (73.3%) rural households.

- Catch the Rain 2023 Campaign creates 10,59,816 Water Conservation & Rain Water Harvesting Structures, 5,88,816 reuse and recharge structures & 12,41,245 watershed development structures; Renovates 2,53,951 traditional water bodies and Establishes 661 Jal Shakti Kendras.

Road Connectivity

Promised

- Construct 60,000 km of National Highways in the next 5 years.

- Double the length of National Highways by 2022.

- Complete the Phase-1 of Bharatmala Project expeditiously.

- Launch Bharatmala 2.0 project

- Bring in new technologies and designs in road construction, operation, and maintenance.

- Become a world leader in e-mobility

Delivered

- The National Highway (NH) network increased by 60% from 91,287 km in 2014 to 1,46,145 km in the year 2023

- The average pace of NH construction increased by 143% to 28.3 km/day in 2014

- Due to COVID-19 & other related challenges, Govt. has extended the deadline for completion of the flagship highway development project Bharatmala Phase-I to 2027-28.

- Among the new technologies being tried are Self-healing concrete, Recycled Plastic Roads, Prefabricated Plastic Roads, and Solar Roads.

- India's EV market is expected to expand at a compounded annual growth rate (CAGR) of 45.5% between 2022 and 2030. The government targets 30% of electric vehicles by 2030.

- 8,738 operational Public EV Charging Stations in India as of June '23

- 14,33,545 electric vehicles registered in India in 2023 (till 12.12.2023)

Railways

Promised

- Convert all viable rail tracks to broad gauge by 2022

- Ensure electrification of all railway tracks by 2022.

- Run high-speed trains and new version trains like Vande Bharat all over the country in the next 5 years.

- Complete the dedicated freight corridor project by 2022.

- Launch a massive program for the modernization of railway stations.

- Equip all main railway stations with WiFi facilities by 2022

Delivered

- During 2004-14, 14,985 RKM of rail track work was done, whereas in the last 9 years (2014-23), 25,871 RKM of track laying work has been done. In the year 2022, 23 per day, 14 km of track will be laid, and this year's target is to achieve 16 km of track per day.

- The Total Broad Gauge (BG) network of 60,814 km has been electrified up to November'2023

- Thirty-five indigenously designed, semi-high-speed Vande Bharat Express trains (70 services) are currently serving people across the country. Six more Vande Bharat trains will be launched soon, making it to 82 services. These trains cover up to 247 districts.

- Dedicated Freight Corridor: Now almost all of EDFC has been completed, and WDFC is about to be completed. 2,513 km were commissioned, i.e., approximately 90 % of DFC has been commissioned.

- EDFC: Ludhiana to Sonnagar (1337 km) completed

- WDFC: 1176 km out of 1506 km from Jawaharlal Nehru Port Terminal to Dadri has been completed

- 1,309 Amrit Bharat Stations have been identified across the nation, with the aim to significantly modernize passenger amenities and improve accessibility & inclusivity of railway stations.

- Six thousand one hundred 8 railway stations across the nation started offering free and high-speed WiFi facilities.

Establishment of New Airports

Promised

- Double the number of functional airports from 101 to 202 in the next 5 years

Delivered

- The number of operational airports in the country has doubled from 74 in 2014 to 148 in 2023 as a result of Govt's initiatives like the Regional Connectivity Scheme – UDAN, launched in 2016, under which 469 routes connecting 74 airports have been made operational.

- Govt is planning to have 200-220 more airports, heliports, and water aerodromes in the next 5 years.

Coastal Development

Promised

- Speedy completion of the Sagarmala program

- Double the country's port capacity in the next 5 years.

- Encourage integrated development of coastal areas, including coastal cities, coastal transport, and coastal industrialization.

- Upgrade the infrastructure for connecting the coast and hinterland.

- Focus on the development of inland waterways for shifting inland cargo movement from road and rail to water transport.

Delivered

- Sagarmala Program - 237 projects worth Rs. 1.22 Lakh Crore have already been completed, 262 projects worth Rs. 2.44 lakh Crore are under implementation, and 310 projects worth Rs. 2.08 Lakh Crore are under various stages of development.

- Bharat currently has 13 major seaports and over 205 minor ports, accounting for the bulk movement of its maritime traffic.

- Improve Coastal Infrastructure - Out of 171 projects, 53 projects worth Rs. 3,310 Cr. have been completed, and 118 projects worth Rs. 7,660 Cr. are under various stages of implementation and development.

- Modi govt's focus on inland water transport has led to the declaration of 111 National Waterways. The cargo movement on these waterways reached a record high of 108.8 million tons in FY22, reflecting a growth of 30.1% compared to the previous year.

- The Inland Vessels Bill 2021 further facilitates the growth of inland water transport, creating a robust multi-modal transport ecosystem and fostering ease of doing business.

Energy

Promised

- Ensuring the right mix of energy which leads to a cleaner environment

- Supplying quality electricity to all consumers.

- Making the state electricity entities financially sound and administratively more efficient

Delivered

- Modi govt has transformed the power sector from power-deficient to power-sufficient by adding 1,94,394 MW of generation capacity.

- Modi Govt is working toward achieving 500 GW of Non-fossil-based electricity generation capacity by 2030.

- About 13.5 GW of renewable energy capacity was added during the calendar year 2023

- India is 4th globally in Renewable Energy Installed Capacity, 4th in Wind Power capacity, and 5th in Solar Power capacity.

- Every village and household has been electrified. The availability of power in rural areas has increased from 12 hours in 2015 to 20.6 hours, and in urban areas, it has increased to 23.8 hours.

- Total legacy dues amounting to Rs. 88,278 crores have been paid by 13 states/ UTs against a total outstanding amount of Rs. 1,39,947 Cr. as of 03.06.2022. Balance legacy dues as of 13.12.2023 is Rs. 51,668 crores; out of these, 13 states opted for loans from PFC / REC (total loan sanctioned is Rs 1,13,737 Cr). Further, 20 states/ UTs were reported to have no outstanding dues.

Digital Connectivity

Promised

- Every Gram Panchayat will be connected to a high-speed optical fiber network by 2022.

Delivered

- A total of 2,50,000 Gram Panchayats (2,07,230 GPs on OFC and 4,351 GPs on satellite) have been made Service in the country.

- WiFi hotspots have been installed in 1,04,674 GPs.

- 6,01,026 Fiber to the Home broadband connections are provided

Healthy India – Determined India

Promised

- Set up 1,50,000 Health and Wellness Centers (HWCs) by 2022.

- Create an essential devices list and a separate pricing policy for medical devices to ensure their accessibility and affordability to the masses.

- Strengthening Health Infrastructure - Set up one medical college or postgraduate medical college in every district through public or private participation by 2024.

- Double the number of MBBS and specialist doctors in the country by 2024 compared to 2014.

- Accelerate the reforms in the paramedical education sector so as to increase the availability of nurses, pharmacists, and other paramedical personnel.

- Immunization and Nutrition - Make the National Nutrition Mission a mass movement and strengthen infrastructure and capacity in all Anganwadis.

- Ensure full immunization coverage for all children and pregnant women by 2022 under the Mission Indra Dhanush program.

- Eliminating Tuberculosis: Special Mission to eliminate TB from India by 2025.

Delivered

- As of 30.11.2023, a total of 1,62,991 Ayushman Arogya Mandir (AAM) {erstwhile Ayushman Bharat – Health and Wellness Centers (AB-HWCs)} have been operationalized.

- Modi govt. approved the policy for the medical devices sector in 2023.

- The policy is expected to help the Medical Devices Sector grow from the present $11 Bn to $50 Bn in the next 5 years.

- Under the PLI scheme for Medical Devices, a total of 26 projects have been approved, with a committed investment of Rs.1206 Cr.

- 157 Government medical colleges have been approved, out of which 108 medical colleges have become functional

- An increase of 82% in medical colleges from 387 before 2014 to 706 in 2023

- An increase of 112% in MBBS seats from 51,348 before 2014 to 1,08,848 in 2023

- There are over 1,200 paramedical colleges in India offering more than 4,400 programs covering various specializations.

- Poshan Abhiyan has now been re-aligned as part of Mission Saksham Anganwadi and Poshan 2.0, along with Anganwadi services and a revised Scheme for adolescent Girls.

- All Anganwadi Centers are equipped with Smartphones and Growth Monitoring devices (GMDs) for Mothers and infants; so far, an amount of Rs.5402 Cr has been released to States/UTs under the Abhiyaan.

- Intensified Mission Indradhanush (IMI) - Over 34 lakh children and 6 lakh pregnant women were administered vaccine doses during the first 2 rounds of the IMI 5.0 campaign across the country

- Govt launched PM TB Free Bharat in September 2022 (TB Mukt Bharat Abhiyaan) - 5,91,491 people have been screened for Tuberculosis, out of which more than 47,189 were referred to higher Public Health Facilities.

Good Governance

Simultaneous Elections

Promised

- One Nation, One Election': Simultaneous elections for Parliament, State assemblies, and local bodies to reduce expenditure and ensure efficient utilization of resources

- Single Voter List - Ensure a common voter list for all elections

Delivered

- In September 2023, the government issued a notification constituting a high-level committee to examine the issue of simultaneous elections. The first meeting was held on 23rd September 2023.

- The government takes appropriate steps in consultation with various stakeholders to make the election process more accountable and transparent.

Corruption-Free Bharat

Promised

- Continue to ensure more effective governance and transparent decision-making.

Delivered

- Govt launched a comprehensive (GGI) report in 2021 with 58 indicators. Many initiatives & reforms across various sectors empowered & delivered corruption-free, transparent governance to the common citizen.

Civil Service and Governance Reforms

Promised

- To achieve "Minimum Government and Maximum Governance."

- Continue to implement the Rashtriya Gram Swaraj Abhiyan

Delivered

- Govt launched a comprehensive GGI (Good Governance Index) report in 2021 with 58 indicators. Many initiatives & reforms across various sectors empowered & delivered corruption-free, transparent governance to the common citizen.

- The RGSA scheme continued further for implementation during 2022-23 and 2025-26 at a total cost of Rs.5911 crore. During 2022-23, 43,36,584 participants were trained.

Police Reforms

Promised

- Formulate a 'Model Police Act' to have a pro-people citizen-friendly police.

Delivered

- Under the Modernization of Police Forces (MPF), a total central financial outlay of Rs.26,275 crore is allocated for the period 2021-22 to 2025-26 to strengthen the criminal justice system further.

- The scheme includes plans to develop operationally independent high-quality forensic sciences facilities in states/Union Territories and to make the police force sensitive and trained in emerging technologies.

- PM Modi's vision of SMART Police -- a force that would be strict and sensitive, modern and mobile, alert and accountable, reliable and responsive, and techno-savvy and trained is being implemented.

Judicial Reforms

Promised

- Simplify law, encourage mediation, and strengthen judicial and court management systems for easier accessibility.

- Making India the Centre of Arbitration

Delivered

- Under the Modi govt. Sponsored Scheme for Judicial Infrastructure, the number of court halls has increased from

15,818 (2014) to 21,271 (2023), and the number of residential units has increased.

- Video conferencing facilities have been enabled between 3,240 court complexes and 1,272 corresponding jails. 689 e-Sewa Kendras have been set up at court complexes.

- From 01.05.2014 to 07.03.2023, 54 Judges were appointed to the Supreme Court. Eight hundred 87 new Judges were appointed, and 646 Additional Judges were made permanent in the High Courts. The sanctioned strength of Judges of High Courts has been increased from 906 in May 2014 to 1114 currently.

- As of 31.01.2023, 843 Fast Track Courts are functional for heinous crimes, crimes against women and children, etc.

- Bharat's first International Arbitration and Mediation Centre (IAMC) was inaugurated in 2021 under the New Delhi International Arbitration Centre Act, 2019 ("NDIAC Act")

International Financial Services Centre Authority

Promised

- Make India a hub of financial services, expedite the enactment of legislation for creating an International Financial Services Centre Authority.

Delivered

- The International Financial Services Centers Authority (IFSCA) is the regulatory body for the Indian Special Economic Zones. It was established in 2020 under the International Financial Services Centers Authority Act 2019. The International Financial

Services Centre (IFSC) is located in Gujarat International Finance Tec-City (GIFT City).

- On May 27, 2020, the IFSCA released its first set of regulations, namely the IFSCA (Banking) Regulations, 2020.

- In July 2023, the International Financial Services Centers Authority (IFSCA) and Climate Policy Initiative - India (CPI) signed a Memorandum of Understanding (MoU) for mutual assistance and cooperation to increase the mobilization of global sustainable capital flows into Bharat.

Implementing Cooperative Federalism Effectively

Promised

- Ensure greater involvement of the states in all aspects of policy-making and governance, thereby strengthening federalism.

- Ensure implementation of the 14th Finance Commission's recommendations.

Delivered

- Prime Minister Shri Narendra Modi stressed the need to leverage cooperative and competitive federalism to achieve all-round development. Over the last 9 years, since 2014, a total of 55 meetings of various Zonal Councils have been held, including 29 meetings of Standing Committees and 26 meetings of Zonal Councils.

- Modi govt. implemented the 14th Finance Commission recommendation - increase the share of states in the center's tax revenue from the current 32% to 42%.

Ease of Living

Promised

- Constitute a Committee for Easing Citizens' Interactions with Government (CECIG).

- Empower citizens and ensure time-bound delivery of public services.

Delivered

- The introduction of Digital India has dramatically reduced the distance between the government and citizens. It has also helped in the delivery of substantial services directly to the beneficiary in a transparent and corruption-free manner.

- Common Services Centers – CSCs are offering government and business services in digital mode in rural areas through Village Level Entrepreneurs (VLEs). Over 400 digital services are being offered by these CSCs.

- Unified Mobile Application for New-age Governance (UMANG) – for providing government services to citizens through mobile. More than 1,570 government services and over 22,000 bill payment services are made available at UMANG.

- E-District Mission Mode Project (MMP): e-District project has been implemented at district and sub-district levels of all States/ UTs, benefiting all citizens by delivering various e-Services. Presently, 4,671 e-services have been launched in 709 districts across Bharat.

- Total digital payment transactions volume increases from 2,071 crore in FY 2017-18 to 13,462 crore in FY 2022-23

Science and Technology

Promised

- Launch a new Science Mission for the development of cutting-edge technologies and future technologies, with a special focus on the Artificial Intelligence mission and Robotic Research Mission.

- Make S&T investment available to 95% of students who attend state government institutions, too, through a National Research Foundation in partnership with states.

- Launch a Language Translation Mission to translate S&T and humanities stream books from English to Indian languages.

- Initiate a genome mission for human health.

- Explore the diversity of our oceans.

- Use technology to transform Waste into Energy and Wealth.

- Fund research projects with private participation

Delivered

- PM Modi's Science, Technology & Innovation Advisory Council (PM-STIAC) has identified 9 national science missions aimed to address major scientific challenges to ensure India's sustainable development, including Mission Quantum Frontier, Artificial Intelligence, National Biodiversity Mission, Mission Electric Vehicles, etc.

- PM Modi launched (Jan 2020) The Indian Science Technology and Engineering Facilities Map (I-STEM), the national web portal for sharing R&D facilities, which was formally launched in January 2020.

- In the first phase, the portal is listed with more than 20,000 pieces of equipment from 1050 institutions across the country and has more than 20,000 Indian researchers. The I-STEM portal facilitates researchers.

- PM Modi launched 'Digital India BHASHINI' in 2022 – This seeks to enable easy access to the internet and digital services in Indian languages, including voice-based access, and help the creation of content in Indian languages.

- The government aims to sequence 10,000 genomes by the end of the year 2023 under the Genome India Project (GIP).

- The Department of Biotechnology, Ministry of Science and Technology has sequenced close to 7,000 genomes, and 3,000 of these are already available for public access.

- The Deep Ocean Mission 2021 is part of the Government of Bharat's Blue Economy initiative.

  Exploration of strategic minerals like cobalt, nickel, copper, and manganese is expected & 11 Potential sites for hydrogen sulfides have been mapped.

- The estimated cost of the Mission is Rs. 4047 Cr for 5 years.

- The "Swachhata" campaign, inspired by Prime Minister Shri Narendra Modi, has generated awareness about the 'waste to wealth' concept. Govt. advocates the Trinity of Artificial Intelligence, Robotics, and Drones in order to segregate waste intelligently and for swift disposal of resultant materials.

- Modi Government has earned a total revenue of Rs.776 crore just by disposing of scrap in the 3 Special Campaigns undertaken by all Government offices across the country in just 3 years.

- The Anusandhan National Research Foundation(NRF) Bill, 2023 - provides high-level strategic direction for research, innovation, and entrepreneurship in the fields of natural sciences, including mathematical sciences, engineering and technology, environmental and earth sciences, health, and agriculture.

- The scheme envisages spending of Rs. 50,000 crores for 5 years, out of which Rs. 36,000 crores, almost 80%, is coming from non-government sources.

Forest and Environment

Promised

- Forest and Environment - Adoption of cleaner practices to make our nation a greener country

- Clean up the 102 most polluted cities under the National Clean Air Plan and reduce pollution in these cities

- Continue providing basic amenities to people living in remote forest areas

Delivered

- National Mission for a Green India (GIM) is one of the 8 Missions outlined under the National Action Plan on Climate Change. It aims to protect, restore, and enhance India's forest cover and respond to climate change by undertaking plantation activities in the forest and non-forest areas in the selected landscapes. A total of Rs 512 crore was allocated for this initiative.

- Nagar Van Yojana (NVY) was launched during the year 2020 for the creation of Nagar Vans in urban areas, which promotes urban forestry by involving local communities, NGOs, educational institutions, local bodies, etc.

- Three hundred 85 projects have been sanctioned with Rs 238 crore.

- The Forest (Conservation) Amendment Act 2023 exempts an area of up to 0.10 ha in forests to provide access to the public for habitation, road/rail, and side amenities. This small exemption will pave the way for tribal children, especially the girl child, to get access to education. It will allow pregnant women and elderly people to access hospitals. It will weaken the hold of extremism as forest dwellers will join the developmental mainstream.

- Prime Minister Particularly Vulnerable Tribal Groups (PVTG) Development Mission. – Aimed to improve socio-economic conditions of the PVTGs families and habitations with basic facilities such as safe housing, clean drinking water, and sanitation, improved access to education, health and nutrition, road and telecom connectivity, and sustainable livelihood opportunities. The mission is supported through the availability of Rs.15,000 crore.

Protecting the Himalayas

Promised

- Provide special financial assistance in the form of a 'Green Bonus.'

Delivered

- The government is implementing 2 national missions: the National Mission for Sustaining the Himalayan Ecosystem (NMSHE) and the National Mission on Strategic Knowledge for Climate Change (NMSKCC). Under these Missions' support is being provided to various Institutions and Universities to carry out R&D studies related to climate change science and adaptation strategies.

Focusing on Island Territories

Promised

- Ensure overall development of the island regions through steps like the Island Development Authority (IDA)

Delivered

- The Home Minister of Bharat is the Chairman of the Island Development Agency, and the CEO of NITI Aayog acts as the convener of IDA and chaired the 6th meeting on January 13, 2020, to review the progress of holistic development of islands (Infrastructure, Jobs, connectivity, better communications)

- In the second phase of IDA, suitable sites in 12 more islands of Andaman & Nicobar Islands and 5 islands in Lakshadweep have been covered.

- Tourism has been identified as a key sector due to its multiplier effect. The government is actively promoting various kinds of tourism, like eco-tourism, heritage tourism, adventure tourism, and monsoon tourism.

- Modi Government has also been focusing on air, road, and sea connectivity in the UTs. A new terminal building of Veer Savarkar International Airport at Port Blair has come up with a cost of about ₹710.00 crore with a capacity to handle 50 lakh passengers per year. 'Azad Hind Fauz Setu' on Humphrey Strait at a cost of ₹203.00 crore has significantly improved the road connectivity in the island UT of A&NI.

Development of Northeastern States

Promised

- Ensure accelerated development of the Northeastern states

- Development of infrastructure and improved connectivity in the Northeastern state

- Protect the unique linguistic, cultural, and social identity of the Northeastern states

Delivered

- Prime Minister's Development Initiative for North East (PM-DevINE) – launched with Rs 6600 Cr. Till 26.12.2023, 9 (9) projects worth ₹855.85 crore have been sanctioned, and 14 projects worth ₹3138.68 crore have been recommended for sanction. In addition, 12 projects worth ₹983.05 crore have been recommended in principle (selected) under PM-DevINE.

- North East Special Infrastructure Development Scheme(Roads) -NESIDS (Roads) - Till now, **10** projects worth ₹552.63 crore have been sanctioned, and 3 projects worth ₹182.54 crore have been selected for sanction. In addition, 21 projects worth ₹1452.87 crore have been recommended for selection under NESIDS (Roads).

- North East Special Infrastructure Development Scheme (Other than Roads Infrastructure)-NESIDS (OTRI) - Under NESIDS (OTRI), the total projects sanctioned are 1548 worth ₹18488.94 crore, out of which 1098 projects worth ₹11250.83 crore are completed and 450 projects worth ₹7238.04 crore are ongoing.

- Schemes of North Eastern Council (NEC) - ₹1778.76 crore was available for new sanction. Till now,195 projects worth ₹857.34 crore have been sanctioned under Schemes of NEC.

- Ambitious Akhaura-Agartala New Rail Line Project inaugurated by PM Shri Narendra Modi and PM of Bangladesh Smt. Sheikh Hasina

- Govt launched the Data Analytics Dashboard; data of 112 schemes across 55 Departments and Ministries are available on this dashboard.

- Govt, in collaboration with AMTRON, launched 5G applications for the NER states; it focuses on healthcare, agriculture, edge computing, and 5G labs.

- The entrepreneurial landscape in the North Eastern Region (NER) has undergone a transformative surge, with 4500+ registered startups and 25 active incubators.

- Priority is being given to niche tourism, including Anthropological Tourism, Tribal Tourism, Folklore Tourism, Mountain Tourism, Handicrafts Tourism, Ethnic Tourism, and tea tourism.

Yuva Bharat - Tomorrow's India

Creating Opportunities for Youth

Promised

- 22 major 'Champion Sectors' were identified as the main drivers of the Indian economy.

- Launch a new scheme to provide collateral-free credit up to ₹50 lakh for entrepreneurs.

- Set up a new 'Entrepreneurial Northeast' scheme to provide financial support for NE states

- Take the number of beneficiaries of Mudra loans up to 30 crores.

- Encourage Startups through the creation of a 'Seed Startup Fund' of ₹20,000 crores.

Delivered

- Modi govt has formulated an 'Action Plan for Champion Sectors in Services' to give focused attention to 12 identified Champion Services Sectors with the allocation of Rs. 5000 Crores.

- Rs 2 lakh crore additional collateral-free credit to MSMEs

- The entrepreneurial landscape in the North Eastern Region (NER) has undergone a transformative surge, with 4500+ registered startups and 25 active incubators.

- For the development of the MSME sector in the East Region, the Modi govt has taken the initiative to identify and nurture potential first-generation local entrepreneurs and provide finance on easy terms to help them set up viable industrial projects with a sanction of Rs 766 crore.

- As of 24.11.2023, out of a total of 44.46 crore loans sanctioned under PM Mudra Yojana (PMMY), 30.64 crore (69%) have been sanctioned to women.

- Fund of Funds for Startups (FFS) Scheme: The Fund of Funds for Startups Scheme was approved and established in June 2016 with a corpus of Rs 10,000 crore.

- Startup India Seed Fund Scheme (SISFS) - Approved for the period of 4 years starting from 2021-22 with a corpus of Rs. 945 crore.

Youth In Governance

Promised

- Incentivise and reward self-organized groups of youth who adopt social assets like schools, hospitals, lakes, public gardens, etc., and ensure their maintenance

- Launch a special awareness and treatment program for de-addiction among youth.

- Support a large-scale internship program for the youth in urban local bodies.

Delivered

- National Youth Corps (NYC): Two National Youth Volunteers are deployed in each block of the country to work as an extended arm of Nehru Yuva Kendra Sangeetha (NYKS) and function as a bridge between the NYKS offices and the Youth Clubs in the conduct of the programs of NYKS. An amount of Rs.5,000/- per volunteer per month is paid as an honorarium.

- Govt. launched YUVA 2.0 - Prime Minister's Scheme for Mentoring Young Authors, an Author Mentorship program to train young and budding authors (below 30 years of age) in order to promote reading, writing, and book culture in the country, and project India and Indian writings globally.

- Govt launched Nasha Mukt Bharat Abhiyaan (NMBA) in 272 most vulnerable districts, under which a massive community outreach is being done with the help of about 8000 youth volunteers. More than 44 Lakh youth have been reached out under this scheme.

- The Urban Learning Internship Program (TULIP) was launched by Modi govt in June 2020. Since its inception, 1,00,000+

students have registered on the portal and have access to more than 27,000 internship opportunities offered by 1800+ urban local bodies across the country.

Sports

Promised

- Recognize the traditional sporting practices and focus on the promotion of specific sports in specific regions

- Encourage 'Khelo India' - Special attention will be given to female and tribal athletes

- Establish a National Sports Education Board (NSEB) for the development of sportspersons.

- A mini stadium in each sub-district

- Ensure that the sporting infrastructure is easily accessible for sportspersons

- Promote the Fit India campaign

Delivered

- Under the Khelo India scheme, there is an exclusive component called "Promotion of Rural, Indigenous, and Tribal Games" for the promotion and development of traditional sports.

- Modi Govt is promoting Indigenous Games and Martial Arts (IGMA) in 09 disciplines under its National Sports Talent Contest (NSTC) scheme, where talented children are selected in the age group of 8-14 years in 10 SAI-adopted Centers.

- Khelo India Women's Leagues organized for various sporting disciplines, which saw the participation of 28,819 women athletes in 240 sports at the zonal and national levels.

- The proposed National Sports Education Board (NSEB) aims to promote sports from the grassroots-level to higher education and then provide opportunities to pursue the same to achieve excellence.

- 1000 Khelo India Centers (KIC) are being set up at the district level to strengthen grassroots-level sports infrastructure in the States and to provide a source of income for local sporting talent by engaging them as coaches in KICs.

- Modi government proposes to build sports grounds in the villages, a mini stadium at every block headquarters besides "one district, one sport." Khelo India centers in 10 districts and is a world-class sports city in the Gorakhpur division.

- Govt has sanctioned 341 sports infrastructure projects under the flagship Khelo India Scheme and National Sports Development Fund (NSDF) with an outlay of Rs 3,165.50 crore.

- Fit India Mission was launched by Prime Minister Shri Narendra Modi on August 29, 2019, to promote physical fitness and health among citizens.

- Fit India Cyclothon got a huge response; around 13 Lakh people participated in the first week of its launch. FIT INDIA Flag, 3-Star, and 5-Star Fit India School certificates - 2.67 lakh schools have been awarded the FIT INDIA Flag

Education For All
Primary and Secondary Education

Promised

- Focus on teachers' training and capacity building

- Initiate a 'Prime Minister Innovative Learning Program' for gifted children

- Establish four-year integrated courses at the National Institutes of Teachers' training.

- Establish Smart Classes

- Open 200 more Kendriya Vidyalayas and Navodaya Vidyalayas by 2024

Delivered

- The Malaviya Mission - Teachers Training Program by the University Grants Commission, which was launched in September 2023 - will ensure continuous professional development and help in building capacities of 15 lakh teachers of HEIs through 111 Malaviya Mission centers across India in a time-bound manner. The Bharat Knowledge System has been included in the program modules.

- The PM Innovative Learning Program 'DHRUV' has been launched to enrich the skills and knowledge of a gifted child and to encourage them to achieve excellence (60 students selected in 1st batch)

- The National Council for Teacher Education has launched the four-year Integrated Teacher Education Program (ITEP). The program has been launched in 57 Teacher Education Institutions from the academic session 2023-24 across the country, said officials.

- 10,778 Information Communication Technology (ICT) labs and 42,311 smart classrooms were approved at the cost of Rs 1,003.8 crore in 2020-21 and Rs 956.8 crore in 2021-22. There are a total of 65,356 ICT labs and 29,178 digital classrooms in India, and 1,19,581 schools have internet facilities.

- Modi govt has given the highest financial approval to Assam, which is Rs 155 crore for 1,859 ICT labs, followed by Tamil Nadu, which is Rs 149 crore for 1,893 labs and smart classes.

- There are currently a total of 1,253 schools in Bharat and 3 abroad in Kathmandu, Moscow, and Tehran. It is one of the largest school chains in the world, with a total of 14,30,442 students (as of 24 July 2022) and 43,888 employees.

Higher Education & Skill Development

Promised

- Increase the number of seats in Central Law, Engineering, Science, and Management institutions by at least 50% in the next 5 years.

- Emphasis on online learning as a major resource for higher education.

- Set up an Arts, Culture, and Music University with a focus on fine arts such as music and dance, a Hospitality and Tourism University, and a Police University.

- Make necessary changes in the legislation to ensure a regulatory overhaul.

- Create 50 more Institutions of Eminence by 2024.

- Motivate more institutions to rank among the top 500 institutions of the world.

- Promote a program for 'Study in India' to bring foreign students to study in Indian institutions.

- Incentivize the industry to collaborate with our scientific labs and technological institutions.

- Provide students access to leading journals free of cost.

- Skill Development – Formulate a 'National Policy for Reskilling and Upskilling'

Delivered

- The number of universities in the nation has witnessed a significant rise from 723 in 2014 to 1,113 in 2023 (5,298 colleges have been built in the last 9 years)

- 43% of universities and 61.4% of colleges are located in Rural Areas. 7 IITs and 7 IIMs were built in the last 9 years.

- NISHTHA – "National Initiative for School Heads' and Teachers' Holistic Advancement" is an integrated Online teacher training program launched in August 2019 (69,715 enrolments so far)

- DIKSHA- One nation, One digital platform for school education (6,068 QR coded-energized textbooks, including 361 NCERT textbooks, 307,475 lakhs e-contents)

- As part of the NEP 2020 Carnatic Music (Vocal) course at the National Institute of Technology Puducherry

- Under the leadership of Prime Minister Shri Narendra Modi, the Government of India is establishing a network of National Forensic Science Universities across the country.

- Rashtriya Raksha University, an Institution of National Importance, Pioneering National Security and Police University of Bharat, was established in 2020.

- Under the new National Education Policy (NEP2020), viewed as an overhaul after 34 years, the 10+2 system of school education will be reworded into the 5+3+3+4 system.

- Govt. plans to increase the number of Institutes of Eminence (IoEs) from the existing 20 to 50.

- 41 Indian universities, 7 more than last year, have made it to the QS World University Rankings 2023. Indian Institute of Science (IISc) Bangalore has grabbed the highest rank at 155.

- Education in India Program is a centralized online portal wherein foreign students can apply to more than 160+ top Indian institutes like IITs, NITs, IISC, etc., that offer 2600+ diverse range of courses across multiple disciplines. Students from more than 136 countries are currently pursuing higher education in Bharat.

- A "National Quantum Mission (NQM)" has been launched at a total cost of Rs.6,003.65 crore for 8 years to seed, nurture, and scale up scientific and industrial R&D and create a vibrant & innovative ecosystem in Quantum Technology (QT)

- National Super Computing Mission (NSM)- under the mission, 28 systems have been commissioned across the nation

- National Digital Library for Children and Adolescents was proposed.

- Indian Institute of Skills formed with 3 key partnerships with IIT Kanpur HAL and DASI.

- The Skill India Initiative (PMKVY) and Skill Hub Initiative (SHI) act as upskilling/reskilling courses for Industrial Training Institute (ITI) pass students and trainers. Around 700 candidates have enrolled.

Women Empowerment
Women-Led Development

Promised

- Continue promoting 'Beti Bachao, Beti Padhao'

- Ensure access to credit for rural women entrepreneurs, SHGs, and women farmers.

- Increase the female workforce participation rate over the next 5 years.

- Ensure that 10% of the material to be sourced for government procurement will be done from MSMEs having at least 50% of women employees in their workforce.

- Strengthen the creche program - Ensure that the number of childcare facilities is increased threefold by 2022.

Delivered

- Govt continued the promotion of "Beti Bacho, Beti Padhao," & the expenditure was Rs 246 crore (2019-2022).

- As of 24.11.2023, out of a total of 44.46 crore loans sanctioned under PM Mudra Yojana (PMMY), 30.64 crore (69%) have been sanctioned to women. Under Stand-up India (SUPI), out of 2.09 lakh loans sanctioned, 1.77 lakh (84%) have been sanctioned to women entrepreneurs.

- Under the National Rural Livelihoods Mission, approximately 9.0 crore women are connected with around 83 lakh women's self-help groups (SHGs)

- National Cooperative Development Corporation is playing a significant role in uplifting women cooperatives.

- Periodic Labor Force Survey Report 2022-23 released Govt on 9th October 2023 shows Female Labor Force Participation Rate in the country has improved significantly by 4.2 percentage points to 37.0% in 2023.

- Govt is implementing Credit Guarantee Scheme for Micro and Small Enterprises through CGTMSE for providing collateral-free loans up to a limit of Rs. 5 crore (w.e.f. 01.04.2023) to MSEs with a guarantee coverage of up to 85% for loans to women. 15.10 lakh guarantees of Rs.65,209 crore have been extended to women-owned MSEs.

- The government aims to establish 17000 Crèches, out of which 5222 have been approved to date. As of 31.10.2023, 2412 Modi Govt-aided Standalone Crèches are operational.

Ensuring Equal Rights

Promised

- Legislate Bills to prohibit and eliminate practices such as Triple Talaq and Nikah Halala.

Delivered

- 1st August 2019 is a historic day in Indian Parliamentary history when The Bill against Triple Talaq was made a Law. There is a decline of about 82 percent in Triple Talaq cases thereafter.

Ensuring a Dignified Life for Women

Promised

- Focus on affordable maternal healthcare services for all women.

- Reduce malnutrition by at least 10% in the next 5 years.

- Ensure that all reproductive and menstrual health services are easily available to all women across India.

- Increase the coverage of Ayushman Bharat to include all Anganwadi workers and ASHA workers.

- Women's security will be given more priority.

- Make gender sensitization courses an essential part of all educational institution's curricula and training modules for public offices.

- Provide skill training and strengthen social security mechanisms for widows of our Martyrs.

Delivered

- Janani Suraksha Yojana (JSY) is a demand promotion and conditional cash transfer scheme for promoting institutional delivery.

- Janani Shishu Suraksha Karyakaram (JSSK) entitles every pregnant woman to free delivery, including for cesarean section, in public health institutions, along with the provision of free transport, diagnostics, medicines, other consumables, diet, and blood.

- Pradhan Mantri Matru Vandana Yojana (PMMVY) 2.0 - incentive amount of ₹6,000 in a single installment following the birth of the second girl child. More than ₹3.11 Crores beneficiaries have been given financial support with a total disbursement of more than ₹14,103 Crores.

- Pradhan Mantri Surakshit Matritva Abhiyan (PMSMA): provides pregnant women fixed day, free of cost assured and quality Antenatal Care on the 9th day of every month (3.94 pregnant women beneficiaries & 19,215 facilities)

- Under Pradhan Mantri Bhartiya Janaushadhi Pariyojana (PMBJP), the government launched Jan Aushadhi Suvidha Sanitary Napkins at Rs. 1/- per pad for women sold through more than 10000 Jan Aushadhi Kendra since inception, until 30th November 2023, over 47.87 crore Jan Aushadhi Suvidha Sanitary Pads have been sold at Jan Aushadhi Kendras.

- Creation of 1,50,000 Health and Wellness Centers (AB-HWCs), now renamed *Ayushman Arogya Mandir,* by upgrading the Sub Health Centers (SHCs) and rural and urban Primary Health Centers (PHCs) in both urban and rural areas.

- NIRBHAYA fund allocations are made for strengthening the safety and security of women in the country. During the financial year 2023-24, Rs 200 crore was allotted under the NIRBHAYA fund.

- The National Council of Educational Research and Training (NCERT) has developed syllabi and textbooks across the subjects to promote gender sensitization in the school curriculum.

- Vocational Training Grant for widows of Ex-servicemen (ESM) has been increased from Rs. 20,000/- to Rs. 50,000/-(one time)

- The Ministry of Petroleum & Natural Gas has reserved an 8% quota for the allotment of LPG distributorship and petrol/diesel retail outlets for defense personnel, which also include widows and dependents of members of the Armed Forces who died in the war.

Ensuring a Dignified Life for Women

Promised

- 33% reservation in Parliament and state assemblies through a constitutional amendment.

Delivered

- The Constitution (One Hundred and Twenty-Eighth Amendment) Bill, 2023, seeking to reserve 33% of seats in Lok Sabha and state Assemblies for women, was passed unanimously by both the Lok Sabha and the Rajya Sabha (Sep 2023)

Inclusive Development
Justice for All

Promised

- Ensure benefits of constitutional provisions of the Scheduled Castes, Scheduled Tribes, and backward classes

Delivered

- By removing Article 370, PM Modi has given the rights of the reservation to hill communities, scheduled castes, scheduled tribes, women, and senior citizens.

Strengthing "Sabka Vikas"

Promised

- Eklavya Model Residential School for (EMRS) and ST or ST community.

- Ensure that the rights of all forest dwellers are fully protected.

- Establish 50,000 'Van Dhan Vikas Kendras' in the tribal areas of the country to ensure the availability of primary processing and value addition for forest produce.

- Ensure occupational health and safety for Safai Karamcharis.

Delivered

- More than 1.2 lakh students are enrolled in 401 EMRS. The number of female students (60,815) in EMRSs exceeds that of male students (59,255). Over 38,000 teachers and support staff are to be recruited for the EMRS.

- Prime Minister launched the <u>Pradhan Mantri Janjati Adivasi Nyaya Maha Abhiyan (PM JANMAN)</u> with a budget of around Rs 24,000 crore for the overall development of Particularly Vulnerable Tribal Groups (PVTGs).

- Scheduled Tribes and Other Traditional Forest Dwellers (Recognition of Forest Rights) Act, 2006 (In short FRA) was enacted by the Parliament to recognize and vest forest rights in the Forest Dwelling Scheduled Tribes and Other Traditional Forest Dwellers. The total number of community rights given till May 2014 was 23,578, whereas, during the period from 2014 to June 2023, 86,621 community rights were given across the country.

- Govt. targeted the establishment of 50,000 Van Dhan SHGs subsumed into 3000 Van Dhan Vikas Kendra Clusters (VDVKCs). In a short span of 2 years, successfully sanctioned 52,976 VDSHGs subsumed into 3110 VDVKCs covering 9.27 lakh beneficiaries & 27 States/UTs.

- The Prohibition of Employment as Manual Scavengers and their Rehabilitation Act 2013, which has come into force w.e.f. 06.12.2013. Under the Swachhta Udyami Yojana of NSKFDC, concessional loans are provided to safai karamcharis, manual scavengers & their dependents.

- Self-Employment Scheme for Rehabilitation of Manual Scavengers (SRMS) - One-time Cash Assistance of Rs. 40,000 per family has been provided to all identified and eligible 58098 manual scavengers.

Ensuring the Welfare of the Poor

Promised

- Bring down the percentage of families living below the poverty line to a single digit in the next 5 years.

- Pucca houses for families living in Kuchha houses by 2022

- Further, widen this cover to provide subsidized sugar (at Rs. 13 per kg per family per month) to these families in line with our motto 'Sabka Saath-Sabka Vikas.'

- Ensure that every Indian has access to banking facilities within a radius of 5 km.

Delivered

- 13.5 crore Indians escape Multidimensional Poverty in 5 years. There was a steep decline in the number of multi-dimensionally poor from 24.85% to 14.96% between 2015-16 and 2019-21.

- Rural areas saw the fastest decline in poverty, from 32.59% to 19.28%

- 118.90 lakh houses have been sanctioned under PMAY-U. Of the sanctioned houses, 113 lakh have been grounded for construction; 75.31 lakh are completed/delivered to the beneficiaries. During the last 3 years, 45.43 lakh houses have been sanctioned, and 39.63 lakh houses have been completed/ delivered to the beneficiaries

- Under Pradhan Mantri Garib Kalyan Anna Yojana (PMGKAY), free food grains to 81.35 crore NFSA beneficiaries for a period of 5 years with effect from 1st January 2024. Modi govt launched sale of 'Bharat' Atta at an MRP of ₹ 27.50/Kg

- More than 50 crore beneficiaries have banked under PMJDY since its inception.

- PMJDY accounts grew 3.4-fold from 14.72 crore in March 2015 to 50.09 crore as of 16-08-2023. Around 56% of Jan-Dhan account holders are women, and around 67% of Jan-Dhan accounts are in rural and semi-urban areas.

Responsive to the Needs of Aspirational Middle Class

Promised

- Further, revise the tax slabs and the tax benefits to ensure more cash and greater purchasing power in the hands of our middle-income families.

- Ensure that our aspirational middle class has access to education, employment opportunities, and suitable urban infrastructure for a better quality of life.

Delivered

- The Union Budget 2023 raised the minimum taxable income to Rs. 3,00,000 from the previous Rs 2,50,000 minimum amount.

- The middle class in Bharat benefited the most from tax reforms brought in by PM Modi-led government. Steps like lowering GST rates of 11.4% from 15.4 %, eventually leading to a saving of more than 18 lakh crore since its launch in 2017

- Twenty thousand crore rupees were saved through affordable medicines available at Janaushadhi Kendras.

- Seven new IITs, 7 new IIMs, and 353 new universities were established.

- The number of medical colleges and AIIMS has increased from 387 to 660 and 7 to 23, respectively, from 2014 to 2023. Similarly, PG seats increased from 31,185 to 65,335 and MBBS seats from 51,348 to 1,01,043 between 2014 and 2023.

- Nine lakh jobs were created through 1 lakh startups working as an additional source of employment for the middle class.

- The number of houses sanctioned increased from 13 lakh during 2004-2014 to 1.2 crore during 2014-2022.

- While the percentage of the middle class in 2014 stood at 26%, this increased to about 31% in 2023.

- Under PM Modi's governance, the per capita income of the nation has almost doubled and currently stands at Rs 1,72,000 as compared to Rs 86,647 in the year 2014-15.

- The share of government health expenditure in total health expenditure increased from 28.6% in FY14 to 40.6% in FY19.

- Thirty-five indigenously designed, semi-high-speed Vande Bharat Express trains (70 services) are currently serving people across the country. Six more Vande Bharat trains will be launched soon, making it to 82 services. These trains cover up to 247 districts.

Commitment to Geographical Equity

Promised

- Ensure that Eastern India is an equal participant in the progress and growth of the nation

Delivered

- Continuation of the North East Special Infrastructure Development Scheme (NESIDS) with an approved outlay of ₹8139.50 crore for the period from 2022-23 to 2025-26 was approved.

- Govt. approved continuation of the 'Schemes of NEC' for the period from 2022-23 to 2025-26 with a total outlay of ₹3202.7 crore.

- Prime Minister's Development Initiative for North East Region (PM-DevINE): A new Central Sector scheme, with 100% Central funding, in the Union Budget 2022-23 with a total outlay of ₹6,600 crore

- The government launched the Data Analytics Dashboard; data from 112 schemes across 55 departments and ministries are available on this dashboard.

- North East Venture Fund (NEVF) developed a dynamic startup ecosystem in the region and extended investment support to 67 startups.

- The entrepreneurial landscape in the North Eastern Region (NER) has undergone a transformative surge, with 4500+ registered startups and 25 active incubators.

Development with Dignity for the Minorities

Promised

- Committed to the empowerment and 'development with dignity' of all minorities (Muslims, Christians, Sikhs, Buddhists, Jains, Parsis, etc.

Delivered

- Pradhan Mantri Virasat Ka Samvardhan (PM VIKAS) Scheme - provided training to 9,63,448 beneficiaries under the scheme.

- Pradhan Mantri Jan Vikas Karyakram (PMJVK) - with the objective of developing infrastructure projects, which are community assets.

- National Minorities Development and Finance Corporation (NMDFC) - disbursed more than Rs. 8,300 Crs. Covering over 22.5 lakh beneficiaries, out of which more than 85% beneficiaries are women.

- Haj Pilgrimage 2023 - For the first time, single ladies were allowed to apply for Haj under Lady Without Mehram (LWM). More than 4000 ladies benefited.

- 1st August 2019 is a historic day in Indian Parliamentary history when The Bill against Triple Talaq was made a Law. There is a decline of about 82 percent in Triple Talaq cases thereafter.

- Skill Development - Rs 1251 crore allocated benefiting 98,240 minority women.

Caring for Elderly

Promised

- Strengthen the Rashtriya Vayoshri Yojana (RVY) to ensure that poor senior citizens in need of aids and assistive devices receive them in a timely manner.

Delivered

- Rashtriya Vayoshri Yojana (RVY) - Total 12 24, 645 devices amounting to Rs. 24,649.98 lacks distributed to 2,99,942 beneficiaries in 265 Camps.

Enabling Divyangs

Promised

- To further the Sugamya Bharat project, conduct continuous accessibility audits and ratings for cities and public infrastructure.

- Prioritize Divyang beneficiaries under the Pradhan Mantri Awas Yojana.

- Anganwadi and the pre-school system will be strengthened to ensure that cases of disabilities are detected at an early stage.

- Offer higher interest rates on fixed deposits by Divyangs.

Delivered

- To provide full legislative cover to the campaign and the right to accessibility, the government enacted the Rights for Persons with Disabilities (RPwD)Act, 2016, which came into force in April 2017

- AIRPORTS – All 35 international and 55 out of 69 domestic airports have been provided with features of accessibility. RAILWAYS – All 709 A1, A & B category railway stations are fully accessible.

- PUBLIC TRANSPORT – Out of 1,45,747 operational buses owned by 62 State Transport Undertakings - 42,348 (29.05%) buses made partially accessible and 8,695 (5.96%) made fully accessible.

- Under Pradhan Mantri Awas Yojana (Urban), 63,000 differently-abled (Divyang) benefited.

- 157.35 crore children have been screened, 10.11 crore children identified with selected health conditions, and 4.73 crore children have been provided secondary/tertiary care.

- 367 District Early Intervention Centers (DEIC) have been made functional throughout the country

- Govt announces 1% interest rate rebate to Divangjan borrowers under NDFDC loan.

Political Resolution on the Matter of Gorkha

Promised

- Recognize the 11 left-out Indian Gorkha sub-tribes as Schedule Tribes.

- Implement the reservation for the Limboo and Tamang tribes in the legislative assembly of Sikkim.

- Work toward finding a permanent political solution to the issue of Darjeeling Hills, Siliguri Terai, and Dooars region.

Delivered

- Govt is evaluating the legal & other formalities before a decision is reached.

- A proposal for the reservation of seats for Limboo and Tamang communities in the Sikkim Legislative Assembly is under consideration by the Government of Bharat.

- On 12th Oct 2021, Modi govt began tripartite talks today with the Gorkha representatives from the Darjeeling Hills, Terai, and Dooars region and the Government of West Bengal.

Ensuring the welfare of the Labor Force

Promised

- **There has been a 42% growth in the National Minimum Wage. We will maintain the same direction over the next 5 years to ensure respectable living conditions for the workers.**

Delivered

- An Expert Group on the fixation of Minimum Wages and National Floor Wages has been constituted by the Government of Bharat in 2021 to provide technical inputs and recommendations on the fixation of minimum wages and national floor wages to the government.

Pension Scheme for all Small Shopkeepers

Promised

- Expand the Pradhan Mantri Shram Yogi Maan-dhan scheme to cover all small shopkeepers.

Delivered

- The National Pension Scheme for Traders and Self-Employed Persons Yojana (Pradhan Mantri Laghu Vyapari Maan-dhan Yojana) is a pension scheme for shopkeepers/ retail traders and self-employed persons that provides a monthly minimum assured pension of Rs 3000/- for the entry age group of 18-40 years.

- It is a voluntary and contribution-based central sector scheme.

- The scheme is in effect from the 22ⁿᵈ day of July 2019 & benefits more than 3 crore small shopkeepers and traders.

Ensuring the Welfare of Artisans

Promised

- Create an umbrella scheme, 'Pradhan Mantri Kalanidhi Yojana,' to allow flexible and customized financial assistance to support traditional arts.

- Credit Support up to Rs.1 lakh (First Tranche) and Rs.2 lakh (Second Tranche) with a concessional interest rate of 5%. The scheme will further provide Skill Upgradation, Toolkit Incentives, Incentives for digital Transactions, and Marketing Support.

Delivered

- Modi govt approved a new Scheme, 'PM Vishwakarma' (Aug 2023), to support traditional artisans and craftspeople in rural and urban India. The scheme is to have a financial outlay of Rs.13,000 crore with 18 traditional trades to be covered in the first instance under PM Vishwakarma's scheme.

Protecting Our Children

Promised

- Comprehensive Child Protection Framework to facilitate the setting up of standards and robust inspection and monitoring of childcare institutions across India

Delivered

- Juvenile Justice (Care and Protection of Children) Act, 2015 - The Act provides for the protection of children in need of care and protection. Also mandated to monitor the function of the Child Care Institutions (CCIs).

- A quantum of sponsorship of Rs.4000/- per child per month is available for Non-institutional Care of children in Need of Care and Protection, and the provision for a maintenance grant of Rs.3000/- per child per month for children living in Child Care Institutions.

Empowering Transgenders

Promised

- Ensure self-employment and skill development avenues for transgender youth

Delivered

- SMILE: Support for Marginalized Individuals for Livelihood and Enterprise – was launched in Feb 2022 for the Welfare of Transgender community and Beggars.

- The sub-scheme - Comprehensive Rehabilitation for Welfare of Transgender Persons provides Scholarships for Transgender Students, Skill Development, Housing (Shelter homes), composite healthcare, Transgender protection cells, and E-services.

Cultural Heritage

Ram Mandir

Promised

- Explore all possibilities within the framework of the Constitution and all necessary efforts to facilitate the expeditious construction of the Ram Temple in Ayodhya.

Delivered

- On November 9, 2019, the Supreme Court unanimously delivered a historic verdict that paved the way for the construction of the Ram Temple at Ayodhya. The consecration ceremony of the Ram Lalla idol at the newly constructed temple was conducted on January 22, 2024.

Conserving Bharatiya Faith and Culture

Promised

- Expand the ongoing PRASAD scheme to conserve and promote all culturally, religiously, and spiritually significant heritage sites.

Delivered

- "Pilgrimage Rejuvenation and Spiritual Heritage Augmentation Drive' (PRASHAD) and 'Swadesh Darshan' (SD) schemes provide financial assistance to State Governments and Union Territory Administrations.

- Modi govt. sanctioned 46 projects under PRASHAD and 76 projects under the Swadesh Darshan Scheme across the country, which includes religious sites.

Conserving Bharatiya Linguistic Culture

Promised

- Constitute a National Task Force to study the status of all written and spoken languages and dialects in India. Revive and promote vulnerable or extinct dialects and languages.

- Promotion of Sanskrit: teaching of Sanskrit is expanded and popularized at the school level. Provide 100 Panini fellowships to researchers and scholars.

Delivered

- "Scheme for Protection and Preservation of Endangered Languages of India" (SPPEL) to promote all Indian Languages, including endangered languages (Rs 45 crore funded)

- The government decided to conduct the government job test in 15 Indian languages so that the language barrier does not let any youth miss the job opportunity. The JEE, NEET, and UGC exams are also being conducted in 12 of our languages.

- To promote the Sanskrit language, there are 15 State Universities and 3 Deemed Universities across the country.

Namami Gange: A Matter of Pride

Promised

- Ensure that the sewerage infrastructure to deal with 100% of the wastewater from the Ganga towns is completed and is functioning effectively.

- Special project covering the villages on the banks of the river for solid and liquid waste management.

Delivered

- Namami Gange Program - A total sum of Rs. 16,011.65 crore was released by the Government of Bharat to the National Mission for Clean Ganga (NMCG) (2014-2023).

- The total treatment capacity along the towns located along the main stem of river Ganga increased to 2589 MLD. Additionally, 910 MLD sewage is treated through East Kolkata Wetland.

- Projects for developing 1104 MLD STP capacity in the towns along the river Ganga main stem have been taken up, which are at different stages of implementation.

- Rejuvenation of river Ganga and its tributaries- A total of 450 projects have been taken up at an estimated cost of Rs. 38,022.37 Crore, out of which 270 projects have been completed and made operational.

Sabarimala

Promised

- Undertake every effort to ensure that the subject of faith, tradition, and worship rituals related to Sabarimala are presented in a comprehensive manner before the Hon'ble Supreme Court.

Delivered

- The Modi govt. believes in the constitutional framework & continues its legal fight supporting the subject of faith, tradition, and worship rituals.

Promoting Yoga Globally

Promised

- Promote Yoga as a vital method to achieve physical wellness and spiritual rejuvenation across the globe.

- Undertake a rapid expansion of Yoga health hubs, Yoga tourism, and research in Yoga.

Delivered

- Responding to a call by our Prime Minister, Shri Narendra Modi, the United Nations General Assembly on 11 December 2014 declared 21st June as the International Day of Yoga.

- **International Day of Yoga:** The 9th edition witnessed unprecedented outreach, setting 2 world records, including a Guinness record for participation at the UN Headquarters.

- The event witnessed an overwhelming response from thousands of Yoga enthusiasts from over 135 nationalities, setting a Guinness World Record for participation by a maximum number of nationalities in a Yoga session. Surat (Gujarat, India) made a Guinness World Record for the largest gathering of people for a Yoga session in one place. More than one lakh people took part in the event.

Bharatiya Cultural Festival

Promised

- An International Cultural Festival every year in 5 different states

Delivered

- G20 Culture Working Group and Culture Ministers Meeting held under India's Presidency; Outcome Document titled 'Kashi Culture Pathway' agreed upon by all G20 Countries

- "Meri Maati Mera Desh-Maati Ko Naman Veeron ka Vandan," a Nationwide Campaign organized to Honor the 'Veers' Who Sacrificed their Lives for the Nation.

- During Bharat's G20 Presidency, Govt hosted the 4th G20 Culture Working Group Meeting on 24-25 August 2023 in Varanasi.

Dharohar Darshan

Promised

- Launch a web-enabled virtual tour of all such locations through 'Dharohar Dharshan-an integrated web portal'

Delivered

- The government launched an alternative livelihood program under the Amrit Dharohar Capacity Building Scheme-2023 to train facilitators, guides, and other tourism service providers to strengthen nature tourism.

Uniform Civil Code

Promised

- Stand to draft a Uniform Civil Code, drawing upon the best traditions and harmonizing them with modern times

Delivered

- Uniform Civil Code - Numerous requests have been received from various quarters regarding the extension of time for submitting their comments. The Law Commission has decided to grant an extension of 2 weeks for the submission of views and suggestions by the concerned stakeholders (July 2023)

Foreign Policy

Vasudhaiva Kutumbakam

Promised

- Strengthen our role as 'first responder' for disaster relief and humanitarian assistance

Delivered

- Bharat has emerged as the first responder in Humanitarian Assistance and Disaster Relief (HADR) at the global level.

- Operation Dost (Feb 2023) - In the aftermath of the devastating earthquakes that struck Turkey, officially the Republic of Türkiye, Bharat demonstrated its commitment to global solidarity.

- Operation Karuna (May 2023) – Assisted Myanmar after Cyclone Sitrang wreaked havoc. Indian Naval ships with emergency relief materials, including medicines, food & shelter, showcased Bharat's dedication to supporting affected communities.

- Despite the complex political situations in Afghanistan and Ukraine, Bharat continued to extend humanitarian assistance.

- In Afghanistan, shipments of wheat, medicines, and other essential supplies were sent throughout the year, emphasizing Bharat's commitment to standing by the Afghan people during challenging times.

- Multiple consignments of humanitarian aid, including medicines and food items, were dispatched to Ukraine, reinforcing Bharat's solidarity with a nation facing the brunt of conflict.

- Operation Kaveri: The Indian Air Force, under Operation Kaveri, airlifted 24,000 kg of humanitarian aid to Sudan and facilitated the safe return of stranded Indians. Operation Kaveri successfully evacuated 3,862 individuals, with 17 aircraft and 5 Indian Navy ships contributing to this extensive humanitarian effort.

Global Coordination on Knowledge and Technology

Promised

- Create an 'International Space Technology Alliance'

Delivered

- Giving credit to Prime Minister Narendra Modi, who opened up India's Space Sector to private players, which has enabled a quantum jump in the last few years.

- Over 189 Space StartUps within a short span of time, Bharat has gained sound footing, and the entire world has begun to acknowledge Bharat's space capabilities.

- With the implementation of the Indian Space Policy 2023, a $44 billion Indian space economy can be achieved by the year 2033.

- Out of 424 foreign satellites launched to date by Bharat, 389 were launched in the last 9 years of the Modi Govt.

Continuous Dialogue with Indians Living Abroad

Promised

- Launch the 'Bharat Gaurav' campaign to increase interaction among the Indian diaspora

- Strengthen the MADAD portal as a single-point avenue for information and services for Indians living abroad.

Delivered

- PM Modi always ensured strong connections, communication & contributions are there from the Bharat diaspora. PM Modi's continuous interest & interaction with all Bharat communities during all his overseas trips have enabled great support for our nation's visibility & growth.

- 17th Pravasi Bharatiya Diwas Convention 2023 - provides an important platform to engage and connect with overseas Indians and to enable the diaspora to interact with each other. Over 3,500 diaspora members from nearly 70 different countries have registered for the PBD Convention.

Combating Terrorism Through Global Forums

Promised

- Taking concrete steps on international forums against countries and organizations supporting terrorism

- Work toward establishing a 'Committee of Nations Against International Terrorism'

Delivered

- The 3rd Ministerial Conference on Countering Financing of Terrorism - No Money for Terror will be held in New Delhi on November 18 and 19 (2022). No Money for Terror Conference will further Bharat's efforts to build understanding and cooperation among nations on this issue.

Deeper Multilateral Cooperation

Promised

- Pursue cooperation against global evils through forums like the UN, the G20, BRICS, SCO, Commonwealth, etc.

Delivered

- Modi govt strongly urged the developed & developing friendly countries to support the early adoption of the Comprehensive Convention on International Terrorism (CCIT) under the UN umbrella, terming it vital to combat the menace of cross-border terrorism.

- During 2022, Bharat held bilateral counter-terrorism consultations through the mechanism of JWG-CT with Australia, the European Union, Italy, Saudi Arabia, Singapore, Tajikistan, the United Kingdom, and Uzbekistan.

- Bharat remained the Chair of the United Nations Security Council Counter-Terrorism Committee (CTC). Bharat hosted a Special Meeting of the CTC in Mumbai and in New Delhi on 28 & 29 October 2022. The meeting was addressed by all members of the Security Council.

- The "Delhi Declaration" on Countering the Use of New and Emerging Technologies was adopted. The declaration expressed the commitment of the international community.

Permanent Membership of the United Nations Security Council

Promised

- Committed to seeking permanent membership in the United Nations Security Council

Delivered

- Bharat strongly advocates an early and meaningful reform of the United Nations to make it better equipped to serve the needs of the world community. In this context, Bharat has called for the expansion of the UN Security Council to make the UN more effective and reflective of contemporary geo-political realities.

- Modi govt. has been actively working along with other like-minded countries to build support among the UN membership for a meaningful restructuring and expansion of the UN Security Council.

- Bharat, in collaboration with Brazil, Japan, and Germany, together known as the G-4, proposed expansion of the membership of the UN Security Council from the present 15 to 25 with the addition of 6 permanent and 4 non-permanent members, including from Asia, Africa, and Latin America.

Strengthening the Diplomatic Cadre and Outreach

Promised

- Establish a full-fledged University of Foreign Policy

Delivered

By 2027, Bharat will be the third-largest economy. A complex world also needs more specialization — the IFS was meant to be a specialized service. The Bharat diaspora is the largest diaspora in the world, with varied needs and interests. To do all this and more, the IFS must grow, spread out, specialize, but integrate and project a new India abroad in the decades to come.

- Modi government approved a proposal (2023) to review and restructure the Indian Foreign Service (IFS), which is expected to create more than 200 additional posts within the next 5 years.

Summary
(Modi Government – Term 2 (2019 – 2024) – Delivered Development)

Generally, for any Government, the consecutive 2nd term in office will give them a good platform (created during 1st term) to start their 2nd term with less challenges. But Modi Govt's 2nd term is the most notable & challenging phase it went through. COVID19 pandemic hit the entire world & even developed Nations struggled to manage. But Our Nation was protected, shielded & saved from the worst pandemic phase because of our Hon'ble Prime Minister Shri. Narendra Modi's commitment to save our Nation & people from this worst pandemic. There were numerous health initiatives, schemes & economic revival programmes launched to bring back our Nation to development path.

Modi Govt's believed in delivering results for our great Nation Bharat. Our Hon'ble People's Prime Minister: A great leader with patriotism in his blood & nation's development in his heart. His only vision "Bharat's Development" & Elevate Bharat as a developed country in the world by 2047.

Under Hon'ble PM Modi people welfare focused Governance, Mother Bharat's pride was restored; every Bharatiya living abroad could feel a sense of pride & value. Every Nation respected Bharat people's contribution, Bharat's vision & supported development efforts under our great people's Prime Minister. Bharat's economic status was held high in spite of the World's worst economic situations. The word "Corruption" was erased. Bharat became top country in "Foreign Direct Investment Destinations". Domestic manufacturing & production were boosted through Make in India, Startup India, Mudra, etc

PM Modi has initiated a visible change in work culture, both in the Executive and Polity. Optimum use of technology is being made to achieve transparency and delivery of services to the common man. A record 13.5 crore people moved out of multidimensional poverty between 2015-16 and 2019-21 as per NITI Aayog's Report.

Our Nation felt healthy and safe, our strong-armed force not only defended but also delivered a strong message when provoked by Nation's enemies. Development & empowerment were equally enabled for the armed forces to boost their morale and to showcase the value for their patriotism and sacrifice. For the first time in History, many welfare schemes were delivered empowering our armed forces

Our patriotic Prime Minister, Shri. Narendra Modi is the only Prime Minister in the World to spend his continuous 10 years of Diwali festival with Nation's armed forces at the border.

Our Hon'ble Prime Minister Shri Narendra Modi had travelled to more than 60 countries as a proud Bharat's Son, who ensured every country listened, respected, participated & contributed to Bharat's growth & development.

Nation is given "PM Modi's Guarantee" for its Future in 2024. My salute for PM Modi for his dedication, commitment, energy, care for culture, braveness to fight corruption, strong friendship with key Nations & limitless love for his family members **"140 crore people of proud Bharat"**

Top 5 Reasons – PM Modi's Guarantee for Future Bharat 2024

◆————————◇————————◆

1. Saved Mother Bharat from COVID-19 Pandemic

Today we & our family members are saved from the worst pandemic in history of 100 years due to 2 reasons.

1. God blessings

2. Modi Govt dedication

March 11: The World Health Organization (WHO) formally designated Coronavirus Disease (COVID-19) as a 'pandemic.'

But Bharat was one of few Nations in the World to take immediate measures much before March 11, 2020

The Government of Bharat has consistently been taking proactive steps to respond to the COVID-19 pandemic and has been bolstering the preparedness of the health system to respond to all aspects of COVID-19 management. Bharat managed to maintain the lowest positivity and mortality rates coupled with one of the highest recovery rates globally during the pandemic. The country's public health efforts were strongly supported by its research and development capacity in developing vaccines against COVID-19.

Under the leadership of Hon. Prime Minister Shri Narendra Modi, the Nation adopted a 'Whole of Government' & 'Whole of Society' approach in a proactive, preemptive & graded manner, thus adopting a holistic response strategy for effective management of COVID-19.

Modi Govt's strategy is containment, relief package, and vaccine administration. These three measures were critical in saving lives and ensuring economic activity by containing the spread of COVID-19, sustaining livelihoods, and developing immunity against the virus.

The government focused on augmenting health infrastructure in terms of Covid related beds, drugs, and logistics, i.e., N-95, PPE kits and medical oxygen, simultaneously up-skilling human resources through Centre of Excellence and deploying digital solutions such as eSanjeevani Telemedicine service, Aarogya Setu, Covid-19 India Portal etc." Equal weightage was given to scaling up the testing infrastructure at an unprecedented rate, exceeding the superlative figure of 917.8 million (91 crore) tests conducted.

Bharat launched the world's biggest vaccination drive, garnering a coverage of 97% of 1st dosage and 90% of the 2nd dosage, administering 2.2 billion (220 crores) dosages in all for eligible beneficiaries. The drive focused on equitable coverage for all; hence, vaccines were provided free of cost to all citizens.

Immediate Response to COVID-19

- The Modi Govt. constituted 11 Empowered Groups on 29 March 2020 on different aspects of COVID-19 management in the country to make informed decisions.

- A three-tier arrangement of health facilities was created for appropriate management of COVID-19 cases (Isolation Centre, Healthcare Centre & Dedicated COVID-19 hospital)

- The location-enabled app Aarogya Setu was launched to help with the monitoring of COVID-19 cases and contact tracing of people who had tested positive or had been in contact with a COVID-19-positive individual.

Bolstering Infrastructure

- Availability of Ventilators across the country with 19,000 Doctors & para-medic trained on them

- The Government has sanctioned 1563 Pressure Swing Adsorption (PSA) oxygen generation plants

- The number of testing labs for detection of Covid-19 has been increased to 3062 labs

- Treatment of COVID-19 is included under Ayushman Bharat –Pradhan Mantri Jan Arogya Yojana (AB-PMJAY)

Financial Assistance to States

- During the F.Y. 2019-20. funds to the tune of Rs.1113.21 crore were released to the States/U.T.s under the National Health Mission (NHM) towards the management and containment of the COVID-19 pandemic.

- Since September 2020, the Union Government has allowed the use of State Disaster Response Funds (SDRF) for various COVID-19-related activities.

- Central Release of Grants in aid for the COVID-19 activities under the ECRP during F.Y. 2020-21 and F.Y. 2021-22 is Rs 8257 crore & Rs 6075 crore.

- The Bharat COVID-19 Emergency Response & Health System Preparedness Package: Phase-II" has also been approved by Modi Govt. with Rs 23,123 crores being implemented from 1 July 2021

COVID-19 Vaccine Manufacturing Capacity

- Corona Virus Vaccine (COVISHIELD) manufactured by M/s Serum Institute of India Pvt., Ltd., Pune, and Corona Virus Vaccine (COVAXIN) manufactured by M/s Bharat Biotech International Limited, Hyderabad.

- The monthly vaccine production capacity of Covishield is approx. 250-275 Million doses per month

- The monthly vaccine production capacity of Covaxin is approx. 50-60 Million doses/month.

- Both companies have achieved close to 90% of their present production capacity.

COVID-19 Vaccination

- World's biggest vaccination drive, garnering a coverage of 97% 1st dosage and 90% of the 2nd dosage, administering 2.2 billion (220 crores) dosages in all for eligible beneficiaries.

Key Highlights

- Under the Vande Bharat Mission, more than 766 flights have been scheduled from various destinations to Indian cities. 11.70 lakh Bharat citizens stranded abroad in various countries due to the COVID-19 pandemic have been flown in on special flights since May 6, 2020. Similarly, more than 1.66 lakh people (foreigners) stranded in Bharat due to the lockdown have been flown out to their home countries.

- Stanford Paper highlights that Bharat was able to save more than 3.4 million (34 lakhs) lives by undertaking the nationwide COVID-19 vaccination campaign at an unprecedented scale.

- COVID-19 Vaccination campaign yielded a positive economic impact by preventing loss of US$ 18.3 billion (Rs 1.56 lakh crore): Stanford Report

- A net benefit of US$ 15.42 billion (Rs 1.27 lakh crore) for the nation after taking into consideration the cost of the vaccination campaign.

- Spending an estimated 280 billion U.S. dollars (As per IMF) through direct and indirect funding had a positive impact on the economy.

- With schemes to support the MSME sector, 10.28 million (1.2 crore) MSMEs were provided assistance, resulting in an economic impact of US$ 100.26 billion (4.90% GDP)

- Under PMGKAY, free food grains were distributed to 800 million (80 crores) people, which resulted in an economic impact of approximately US$ 26.24 billion.

- Under PM Garib Kalyan Rozgar Abhiyan, 4 million (40 lakhs) beneficiaries were provided employment, which resulted in an overall economic impact of US$ 4.81 billion.

2. Ram Mandir in Ayodhya

The Ram Mandir "Pran Pratishtha", a historic ceremony of the 21st century, happened on 22nd January 2024 at Ayodhya.

Hon'ble Prime Minister Shri. Narendra Modi presided over the 'Pran Pratishtha' rituals at the Shri Ram Janmabhoomi Temple after concluding his 11-day fasting & visits to several temples ahead of the ceremony. Rashtriya Swayamsevak Sangh (RSS)

Chief Mohan Ji Bhagwat, Hon'ble Uttar Pradesh Chief Minister Yogi Adityanath and Hon'ble Governor Anandiben Patel were present inside the sanctum sanctorum during the rituals.

Ram Mandir – The symbol of Bharat's cultural, spiritual & traditional heritage.

Ram Lalla has regained the lost glory after the struggle of 500 years. Lakhs sacrificed their lives, and after numerous protests, Bhagwan Shri Ram returned to his original birthplace.

The invader mindset does not simply seek to capture and conquer countries. It seeks pleasure in causing deep fractures to the pride and glory of a great cultural society. Mughal ruler Babur's commander Mir Baqi destroyed Ram Mandir in Ayodhya & constructed a mosque just to express his gratitude to his master. His intention was to crush the symbol of Bhartiya faith, pride & legacy.

Soon after independence in 1947, there was a great opportunity for the political leadership & Government to bring our lost glory & identity. But this did not happen & we waited for 77 years (since 1947).

The struggle for Ram Janmabhoomi is a symbol of persistence and vigour of the Hindu society. Invaders defeated the rulers, converted some people and divided the land, but the Hindu society never gave up the civilisational spirit of this nationhood. For the last 1500 years, the freedom fighters have been clear about the idea of Swaraj. It was never about just political independence but reclaiming that spiritual identity with freedom.

The idea of Ram Rajya always inspired us to fight against evil. Saving the idea of Bharat, which believes in respect and acceptance of all ways to be true, from the religious supremacist ideology, was the true spirit behind this long and continuous struggle.

With a massive mandate & majority in 2014 for PM Modi, everyone's hope & confidence were further strengthened for Ram Mandir. Prime Minister Modi considers & worships our "Temple of Democracy – The Constitution". The Modi Govt's belief & respect for the constitution deserve a great salute.

The five judges' bench of the Supreme Court of India gave a unanimous landmark verdict on 9th November 2019 favouring temple construction. On 5th August 2020, Ram Mandir's Bhoomi Pujan was performed by Hon'ble Prime Minister Shri. Narendra Modi.

The architectural inspiration for Ram Mandir seamlessly blends elements from both North & South Bharat temple styles, lending it a distinctive pan-Bharat appeal. Non-usage of steel and concrete in Ram Mandir's construction was beyond imagination in modern-day construction. The complete Ram Mandir would be an engineering marvel capable of withstanding the harsh climate and being earthquake resistant for at least 1000+ years.

The entire architectural layout of the Ram Mandir complex adheres to the principle of "Aathmanirbhar Bharat (Self Reliance), incorporating essential features like sewage plants, water treatment facilities and a dedicated power line.

Larsen & Toubro (L&T) took the responsibility for temple construction, and Tata Consulting Engineers (TCE) played the role of project supervision. Both L&T and TCE are contributing to this project voluntarily. Various other scientific and engineering institutions participated immensely, such as IIT- Madras, IIT – Guwahati, IIT- Delhi, IIT – Bombay, IIT – Kanpur,

CBRI Roorkee, NGRI Hyderabad, Institute of Rock Mechanics – Bengaluru and NIT Pune towards different stages of research, construction & planning of the project.

We all should take a moment to thank these great organizations & their employees for their dedication & contribution.

Bharat's history is re-written with the Ram Lalla's Pran Pratishtha in the reconstructed temple. We are fortunate to witness this momentous occasion. The magnanimous celebrations of this occasion with religious and cultural fervour, not just in Bharat but across the globe, signify that this is not a political event. Pran Pratishtha of Ram Lalla is the beginning of a renewed, reenergized Bharat.

Every Ram bhakta will have to contribute to realising Ram Rajya. As the Ram Lalla reclaims His birthplace, it is the occasion of grand celebration. It is also a moment to make a collective resolve for the coming generations – to build a righteous Republic of Bharat.

3. Removal of Article 370

Since 1947, Jammu & Kashmir has been one of the most critical regions of Bharat, having borne the brunt of external aggression & terrorism for seven decades. For many of us, "Article 370" itself may look alien & a puzzle word till the Modi Govt brings up the importance of Nation Integration. It is so unfortunate to see how such a key Nation integration priority was not given focus by previous governments for many decades.

BJP is the only true Bharat political party since its creation, continuously keeping "Abrogation of Article 370" in its key agenda & manifesto.

Background

Jawaharlal Nehru's disastrous support & pathetic reliance on Sheikh Abdullah (The grandfather of Omar Abdullah of J&K) as a counterweight to Maharaja Hari Singh of Jammu & Kashmir and his willingness to play along with Mountbatten on the great game only added huge confusion. In 1947, against this backdrop of chaos and instability, the people of Jammu & Kashmir inherited a worse situation. If Nehru had not supported Sheikh, the accession of Jammu & Kashmir to Bharat could have perhaps happened in August 1947 instead of October 26, 1947.

Like all other States, it was a constitutional process of integration which was halted due to the intrusion from Pakistan's side and subsequent war. Moreover, Nehru took the J&K issue to the United Nations, which was not necessary.

The insertion of an extraordinary temporary provision of Article 370 and delaying accession for handing over the reins to Sheikh Abdullah, both blunders initiated by Jawaharlal Nehru, created a strange situation in a democracy. A country governed by the same constitution had two Constitutions, two Prime Ministers and two flags.

Article 370 of the Constitution was introduced to serve two purposes.

- A transitional purpose, as an interim arrangement until the Constituent Assembly of the State was formed

- Temporary purpose, as an interim arrangement, because of the situation arising out of the war being faced by the State.

In the name of Article 370 in J&K, It was a systematic murder of democracy, manipulating the temporary and transitional cause as a 'permanent' 'special' status. Nationalist forces of Jammu-Kashmir and the rest of Bharat consistently opposed and fought against such undemocratic provisions.

Impact

Forty-two thousand people have been killed in Jammu and Kashmir because Article 370 used to promote the sentiment of separatism, and due to this, terrorism arose there.

Criticizing the Bharat Flag was not an offence in the state, and the rules of the Supreme Court were not applicable.

If a Kashmiri girl married any man outside J&K, she lost her citizenship. And if she married any Pakistani, then that man used to get J&K citizenship. The RTI Act was not applicable to J&K. No one outside J&K could buy land over there. Financial emergencies were not applicable to J&K. & no one from outside could get and settle into J&K. Employment opportunities were very low in J&K, and hence, a lot of youth were heading towards terrorism. Low GDP was there, and corruption was very high – 3 Families enjoyed power under Article 370.

Modi Govt Steps

On the 5th of August 2019, Prime Minister Shri Narendra Modi Ji took a visionary decision to abrogate Article 370 from Jammu and Kashmir. On 11th December 2023, the Hon'ble Supreme Court, with a 5-judge constitution bench, unanimously upheld the Modi government's decision to remove Article 370.

After the abrogation of Article 370, the rights of the poor and deprived have been restored, and separatism and stone pelting are now things of the past. The people of J&K were empowered with record welfare schemes covering farmers, women, children, youth & poor people.

Transformation of Jammu & Kashmir under PM Modi

- All Central laws are enforced in the Union Territory of J&K with a 3-tier Panchayati raj system established for the first time in the history of J&K.

- Out of 53 projects under PM's development package, 32 projects worth 58,477 crore completed

- 10% reservation was provided to the Economically Weaker Section (EWS), and 100% of J&K villages achieved open Defection Free (ODF) status.

- 3.84 lakh houses are sanctioned under the PM Housing scheme; 13.54 lakh tap water connections are provided under the Jal Jeevan Mission.

- 12.53 lakh free LPG gas connections provided to poor women under Ujjwala Yojana

- 82.22 lakh beneficiaries under free healthcare scheme (AB-PMJAY-SEHAT)

- 8,086 km of rural roads were constructed in just four years under PMGSY

- Seven new Govt Medical Colleges, 50 new degree Colleges, 28 B.Sc. nursing colleges and 19 B.Sc. paramedic Colleges were added. IIT Jammu, IIM Jammu and AIIMS Jammu are now operational.

- 31,830 vacancies in Govt. sector have been filled since August 2019, with 7.4 Lakh self-employment opportunities created (since 2021)

- Rs 2,517 crore was directly credited to the bank accounts of 12.55 lakh farmers under PM KISAN.

- There has been a 70 per cent reduction in terrorist incidents in just four years of abrogation of Article 370. From 2004 to 2014, a total of 2829 security personnel and civilians were killed in Kashmir, while from 2014 to 2023, 891 security personnel and civilians lost their lives, which is 70 per cent less than before.

- Handloom and Handicraft Exports doubled from Rs. 563 Crore in 2021-22 to Rs. 1116.37 Crore in 2022-23.

- Modi Govt. has notified a New Central Sector Scheme for Industrial Development of Union Territory of Jammu & Kashmir on 19.02.2021 with an outlay of Rs. 28,400 Cr to boost industrial development.

4. Empowerment of Scheduled Caste (S.C.) & Scheduled Tribe (S.T.) Communities

As per Census 2011, the population of S.C. & S.T. are 16.6% & 8.9% across our nation Bharat. Under PM Modi, Dalits, tribals, and backward classes are getting the maximum benefits from the government's welfare schemes, giving their "rightful dignity".

The vision of PM Modi is to build an inclusive society wherein people of the S.C. & S.T. can lead productive, safe and dignified lives with adequate support for their growth and development. It aims to support and empower people through programmes of educational, economic and social development and rehabilitation wherever necessary. For the first time in history, record welfare schemes were delivered.

Hon'ble PM Modi – A true follower of Dr Ambedkar & his vision of self-reliant Bharat is being carried forward by him.

PM Modi is the first PM to turn Dr Ambedkar's vision of social reform into reality.

The young Bharat was connected to Dr Ambedkar by PM Modi. Dr Ambedkar International Centre was opened in 2017. Panchteerth – Paying tribute to Dr. Ambedkar by developing places associated with his life (His birthplace in Mhow, his residence during studies in the UK, Deeksha Bhoomi where he embraced Buddhism, Mahaparinirvan Sthal in Delhi where he attained parinirvan, His memorial, Chaitya Bhoomi in Mumbai.

The Modi government strengthened the Scheduled Castes and the Scheduled Tribes (Prevention of Atrocities) Act and ensured greater protection for S.C./STs.

PM Modi has immense respect, value, and care for S.C. & S.T. people. He believes that empowerment & value needs to be given to SC/ST. For the first time in our history, the consecutive two terms of Govt, the Hon'ble Presidents of Bharat were chosen from SC & S.T. (Former President Shri. Ram Nath Kovind & The Hon'ble President Smt. Droupadi Murmu).

Scheduled Caste Empowerment

- National Scheduled Castes Finance and Development Corporation (NSFDC) - providing subsidized interest rate loans to Scheduled Castes with an annual family income of up to Rs. 3.00 lakhs for income-generating projects and educational purposes.

- As of June 30, 2023, NSFDC has released an amount of Rs. 7648.89 crores for approximately 85.90 lakh households under credit-based schemes. NSFDC has sanctioned Rs. 274.26

crores for Skill Training Programmes, benefiting 188,727 beneficiaries.

- National Fellowships for S.C. Students (NFSC) – A budget of Rs 2099 crore was allocated to benefit more than 19,500 students (from 2014 to 2022)

- Pradhan Mantri Anusuchit Jaati Abhyuday Yojana (PM-AJAY) - The budget outlay of the scheme for F.Y. 2023-24 is Rs. 2050 crore, and the scheme aims to reduce poverty of the S.C. Communities by the generation of additional employment opportunities through skill development, income generation and related infrastructure development.

- Mudra Scheme – Out of 44.46 crore loans, 10.22 crore loans were given to SC/ST.

- Scholarships of Rs. 369.03 Cr released for 18,32,628 SC student beneficiaries under the Pre-Matric Scholarship scheme (2023)

- Scholarships of Rs. 3546.34 Cr were released for 34,58,538 SC beneficiaries under the Post-Matric scholarship scheme for S.C. students (2023).

- 2564 SC students admitted to 142 private residential schools affiliated by CBSE/state boards for the academic session 2023-24 under the SHRESHTA scheme.

- National Overseas Scholarship for S.C.s (NOC) – A total of 107 students were awarded in 2023 alone.

- Significant 44% increase in enrolment of S.C. students since 2014-15 (66.23 lakh in 2021-22 from 46.07 lakh in 2014-15)

- Notable increase of 51% in enrolment of Female SC Students in 2021-22 (31.71 lakh), compared to 2014-15(21.02 lakh)

- Standup India (Loans up to 1 crore) for SC/ST & Women entrepreneurs - 47,073 (approx) borrowers benefited.

Scheduled Tribe Empowerment

"India will prosper when our tribal communities prosper; the welfare of tribal communities is our foremost priority," said PM Modi.

For the first time in the country after independence, the art and culture of the tribal society and their contribution to the freedom movement and nation-building are being remembered with pride, and they are being honoured on a grand scale.

- More than 1.2 lakh students are enrolled in 401 Ekalavya Model Residence Schools (EMRS). The number of female students (60,815) in EMRSs exceeds that of male students (59,255). Over 38,000 teachers and support staff are to be recruited for the EMRS.

- Prime Minister launched the Pradhan Mantri Janjati Adivasi Nyaya Maha Abhiyan (PM JANMAN) with a budget of around Rs 24,000 crore for the overall development of Particularly Vulnerable Tribal Groups (PVTGs).

- Scheduled Tribes and Other Traditional Forest Dwellers (Recognition of Forest Rights) Act, 2006 (In short, FRA) was enacted by the Parliament to recognize and vest forest rights in the Forest Dwelling Scheduled Tribes and Other Traditional Forest Dwellers.

- The total number of community rights given till May 2014 was 23,578, whereas, during the period from 2014 to June 2023, 86,621 community rights were given across the country.

- Substantial increase of 65.2% in enrolment of S.T. students in 2021-22(27.1 lakh), compared to 2014-15(16.41 lakh)

- Remarkable 80% increase in the enrolment of Female S.T. Students in 2021-22 (13.46 lakh) since 2014-15 (7.47 lakh)

- The budget outlay for the Ministry of Tribal Affairs in F.Y. 2023-24 increased by 70.69% to Rs. 12461.88 cr. Compared to F.Y. 2022-23 (RE)

- Rs.1,17,943.73 crore allocated to the Development Action Plan for Scheduled Tribes (DAPST) for F.Y. 2023-24

- Ministry of Tribal Affairs disbursed scholarships to 32.22 lakh tribal students through DBT from 1st April 2023 to 27th Dec 2023

- 23.43 lakh land titles totalling over 1.8 crore acres distributed up to 31.10.2023 under the Forest Rights Act

5. Empowerment of Minorities

The Modi Government implements various schemes for the welfare and upliftment of minorities, especially the economically weaker and less privileged sections of society, through various schemes for socio-economic and educational empowerment. Many historic welfare benefits were delivered in the last ten years of good governance under PM Modi›s leadership.

In order to ensure that the benefits of the schemes implemented for minorities actually reach the intended beneficiaries, the scholarship amount/ stipend/ financial assistance under various schemes of this Ministry, including skilling, is released directly into the account of beneficiaries through Direct Benefit Transfer (DBT) mode.

- The Govt is implementing the Prime Minister's New 15 Point Programme for the welfare of Minority Communities.

- Pradhan Mantri Virasat Ka Samvardhan (PM VIKAS) Scheme - provided training to 9,63,448 beneficiaries under the scheme (2023)

- Pradhan Mantri Jan Vikas Karyakram (PMJVK) - with the objective to develop infrastructure projects, which are community assets – 49,000 major projects sanctioned

- National Minorities Development and Finance Corporation (NMDFC) - disbursed more than Rs. 8,300 Crs. Covering over 22.5 lakh beneficiaries, out of which more than 85% beneficiaries are women

- Haj Pilgrimage 2023 - For the first time, single ladies were allowed to apply for Haj under Lady Without Mehram (LWM). More than 4000 ladies benefited.

- 1st August 2019 is a historic day in Indian Parliamentary history when The Bill against Triple Talaq was made a Law. There is a decline of about 82 per cent in Triple Talaq cases.

- Skill Development - Rs 1251 crore allocated benefiting 98,240 minorities women (2019-2022)

- Under PM Modi's education scholarship programme, 83 lakh poor students benefited (largely Muslims followed by Christians) in just three years.

- Skill Development schemes for Women of Minority Communities – More than Rs 1028 crore released for three years (2019-2022).

- Under the PM Housing for All (rural) scheme, 30% of beneficiaries are Muslim women (out of 2.94 crore beneficiaries)

- 33% of Muslim farmers benefited from the PM SAMMAN NIDHI scheme (out of 11.27 crore beneficiaries)

- Till 2014, only 4.5 per cent of Muslims were government employees, and the figure has gone up to 10.5 per cent in the last nine years.

- Mudra Scheme – Out of 44.46 crore loans, 13.33 crore loans were given to Muslims.

- More than five crore education scholarships are given to minority communities. 50% of beneficiaries are female students.

- Poor Muslim girl children's school dropout ratio reduced from 70% (2014) to less than 30%.

- PM Shaadi Shagun Scheme - Excusive for Muslim women. The government will provide the selected and deserving candidates with a sum of Rs. 51000 during the time of their marriage for graduated women.

- About 22 to 37 per cent beneficiaries of "Mudra Yojana", "Jan Dhan Yojana", "Ayushman Bharat Yojana", "Kisaan Samman Nidhi", "Ujjwala Yojana", "Swacch Bharat Mission", drinking water and electricity schemes belong to the weaker and backward Minorities.

Bharat's relations with the Islamic nations are better than ever before. PM Modi's personal diplomatic outreach has yielded great results for Bharat & the Muslim nations appreciate the development & good governance of PM Modi. For the first time in history, our PM received the highest civilian awards from the list of Muslim nations below.

- In April 2016, during his visit to Saudi Arabia, Prime Minister Narendra Modi was conferred Saudi Arabia's highest civilian honour- the King Abdulaziz Sash.

- PM Modi was bestowed the State Order of Ghazi Amir Amanullah Khan – the highest civilian honour in Afghanistan.

- In 2018, when Prime Minister Narendra Modi paid a historic visit to Palestine, he was awarded the Grand Collar of the State of Palestine Award.

- In 2019, the Prime Minster was awarded the Order of Zayed Award. This is the highest civilian honour of the United Arab Emirates.

- Order of the Distinguished Rule of Nishan Izzuddin- the highest honour of the Maldives awarded to foreign dignitaries was presented to PM Modi in 2019

- PM Modi received the prestigious King Hamad Order of the Renaissance in 2019. The honour was conferred by Bahrain.

- Prime Minister Narendra Modi received the highest state honour of Egypt - 'Order of the Nile' - from President Abdel Fattah El-Sisi.

Conclusion

"Hindu Dharma" – *"Hindu" signifies all that is Sanatan, or Eternal; "Dharma" means "That, which sustains". Hindu Dharma signifies all that which eternally upholds everything: an individual, a family, a community, a society, and even nature.*

– Dr Mohan Ji Bhagwat during World Hindu Congress (2023)

Our ancient ancestors showcased the value of **"Krinvanto Vishvam Arayam"**, which means "we shall make the entire world excellent; **"Vasudhaiv Kutumbakam"** means the entire world is one large family.

Thousands of years back, this was our great Nation Bharat's identity & contribution to the entire world.

Our Hon'ble Prime Minister Shri. Narendra Modi believes, worships, follows & delivers "Hindu Dharma" to our nation & entire world through his good governance model.

2024 is not election for BJP, 2024 is not election for PM Modi. 2024 is the election for OUR FUTURE. We need to showcase to the entire world that we, 140 crore people, strongly support PM Modi & his dedication to our nation's progress. This will empower our nation to rise to the next level.

We all are measured against what we promise & the delivery of the promises. Modi Govt, in the last 10 years, has delivered many welfare schemes, initiatives, programmes, and projects that transformed & empowered our people, especially the poor. PM Modi has been working continuously for the past 23 years with a "Nation First & Nation Development" attitude.

Prime Minister Modi plays seven key roles for our nation. The roles are:

1. **As a son of the poor people**

2. **A caring father for children & women**

3. **As a guide for youth**

4. **As a patriotic soldier**

5. **As a dedicated karyakarta**

6. **As a reformer**

7. **Bharat's International leader**

A gift is required to be delivered to 140 Cr people of Bharat for his ten years of dedicated good governance. This idea made me write this book as a gift to all our people who had supported our Hon'ble Prime Minister in every step of initiatives, challenges & transformation.

Bharat Mata Ki Jai.

9 798892 776141